On *the* Money!

Additional copies of this book are available from the publisher. Discounts may apply to large-quantity orders.

Address all inquiries to:
ASR Philanthropic Publishing
P.O. Box 782648
Wichita, Kansas 67278
Telephone: 316.634.2100
Facsimile: 316.630.9993
email: info@ASRpublishing.com
Web site: www.ASRpublishing.com

Other books on philanthropy by Robert F. Hartsook include:
Closing that Gift!
How to Get Million Dollar Gifts and Have Donors Thank You!
Getting your Ducks in a Row!
Nobody Wants to Give Money Away!

Edited by Denise Rhoades
Cover design by Lori Cox
Photograph of Bob Hartsook by Kenny Barnes
Lensic Photograph by Robert Reck Photography (Albuquerque, N.M.)

2nd Printing in the United States of America by Mennonite Press, Inc.

ISBN: 0-9663673-6-7

On *the* Money!

Bob Hartsook

ASR PHILANTHROPIC PUBLISHING

Table of Contents

ON THE MONEY!

On the Money!

DEDICATION

I have dedicated all my books to my son, *Austin Hartsook*. While I want to continue this tradition, I also want to acknowledge three other children who bring joy to my life. Austin's sister, *Rachel Cox*, and brother, *Keith Cox*, are very important to me. Most recently, I became godfather to *Luc Hoch*, the son of my best friend and his wife, Bill and Karen Hoch. Luc, now 2 years old, is full of sweetness and personality.

I dedicate this book to my son, Austin, and to these three other wonderful children.

FORWARD

A client, Joanna Sebelien, director of fund development at Harvesters—The Community Food Network, a major food bank, gave me one of my greatest compliments: "When I read your books, it is just like hearing you tell a story in person. It sounds like you."

If you have read any of my other books, you probably are familiar with my basic philosophy of fundraising. Money is practically limitless. Need is practically limitless. What is limited are the people with the confidence to help make the right connections. This book is my fifth and represents the work of many people. Most of these stories, highlighting successful fundraising campaigns, come from clients and others who have proven they have enough confidence and heart to help make the right connections. Their consultants, staff, volunteer leadership and communities have made many sacrifices in order to be successful in changing people's lives.

I would like to thank all the consultants, agencies and institutions that have given of their time to connect with us and guide the writing of this book. Specifically, I extend my appreciation to Tami Druzba for her work on this book while handling other company business; Denise Rhoades as my editor who has supported me in all my books; and Shelly Chinberg, my longtime friend and colleague, who makes sure these books reflect the best of what we have to offer. Finally, I am grateful to my friend and mentor, Art Frantzreb.

Perhaps these stories make it all sound too simple, too easy, too mechanical. Therefore, I am including a section on "How to Use This Book" that will, I hope, help you extract the profound lessons of fundraising from these simple campaign stories.

On the Money!

Fundraising is not an occupation; it is an opportunity to serve. Fundraising is not a chance to be somebody special; it is a chance to do something special. Fundraising is not about convincing someone to do something they don't want to do; it is about service. It is not about self; it is about changing lives.

For our clients and friends, we always want to be "On the Money!"

HOW TO USE THIS BOOK

Lack of confidence is the most significant barrier to success in major gift and campaign fundraising. And confidence only comes from one source—raising money.

We can talk about the success of major universities, museums, social service agencies, etc., yet the first thing you may think is "… but our organization is so different from a university, museum, social service agency, etc." The truth is, we can all learn from the achievements of others. There are lessons to be gained if we take the time to consider fundamental truths about fundraising.

This book is dedicated to illustrating a variety of funding accomplishments achieved by wonderful, dynamic and effective organizations. These are great groups not normally featured in national fundraising journals. We have provided a showcase for these fundraising superstars.

Perhaps you are already asking, "Why should I read this book? How will it help me?"

First, think about the kind of institution you serve. Sounds like an easy question, right? Sure, you work for an educational institution, a social service agency, a youth development organization or some other sector, right? But look beyond the obvious. What kind of organization are you financially? What is your budget? What kind of organization are you when it comes to need? Could you use a larger endowment, do you need to raise capital, or can you sustain your operating expenses for the next year? Is your group located in a large city or in a small town? These questions also help define who you are as an organization.

On the Money!

Second, thumb through the Table of Contents or Index and locate stories—even from organizations outside your sector—that appear to match your organization on other points of interest including financial status, need, location and so on.

Third, think about the fundraising opportunities and challenges you face right now. Are you blessed with a wealthy and highly recognized board, or is your leadership a group of deeply dedicated, but little-known volunteers? Are you located in a leased building, or do you own a facility that could use some renovations? Common strengths and weaknesses will also help you discover stories you can relate to, learn from and appreciate.

Fourth, you might start by flipping through the stories and glancing down at the lessons referred to as *Consultant's Tips*. See if any apply to your situation. This will be a clue to determining which stories you want to read first.

Finally, share this book with volunteers. Success stories can stir up enthusiasm for fundraising, fundraising can generate money, raising money builds confidence, and confidence can be contagious. All this, just from reading a book!

The key to success in fundraising is paying close attention to the lessons life brings your way. May this book serve as one of those beneficial guides.

CHAPTER ONE

DREAM A BIG DREAM

"You are soliciting individuals . . . talk to individuals."

—*Harry Beckwith*

Santa Fe Christian Schools
Solana Beach, California

CAMPAIGN NAME: "Aspiring Beyond"

CAMPAIGN TASK: To make major renovations and upgrades to virtually every building on campus; to build a new, state-of-the-art library and technology center; and to establish an endowment for teachers.

ORIGINAL CAMPAIGN GOAL: $8 million

AMOUNT RAISED: $10 million

LENGTH OF CAMPAIGN: 24 months

HEADMASTER: Jim Hopson

DIRECTOR OF DEVELOPMENT: Chuck Leslie

CAMPAIGN HIGHLIGHT:

Like many nonprofits, there was a time when Santa Fe Christian Schools' (SFCS) financial priorities included keeping the lights on. Teachers considered the job a "ministry," but the school very much wanted to pay them more than missionary salaries. What SFCS needed was more than an influx of money; it required a new mind-set. By setting long-range goals that focused on the mission and elevated the school's stature, the organization was successful in attracting million-dollar support for SFCS.

MISSION:

To create an academic, intellectual and social environment that enables outstanding education in the context of the Biblical truth of Jesus Christ.

HISTORY:

Santa Fe Christian Schools, founded in 1978, was originally built as a hotel in the 1940s. The building was used as a military academy in the 1960s before its transformation into a school. The school was first part of the Christian Unified School District, but became an independent, nonprofit Christian school in 1985.

THE CAMPAIGN FOR SANTA FE CHRISTIAN SCHOOLS:

Santa Fe Christian Schools (kindergarten through 12th grade) is an independent college preparatory school system working in partnership with parents to "develop tomorrow's Christian leaders."

In the late 1990s, the school went through a major change. Prompted by the leadership of John Couch, organizational vice president with Apple computers, a new level of good business and management practices gave the school renewed vision.

The school's board of directors brought in a new headmaster, clearly defined the mission, stepped up the educational standards and, as a result of this cumulative effort, raised their sights for what the campus could become.

> *"The need for a major campaign seemed obvious to everyone. When I talked about an upcoming campaign, no one asked, 'Why are we doing this?' The climate was right."*
>
> —CHUCK LESLIE
> DIRECTOR OF DEVELOPMENT

Prior to the campaign, Chuck Leslie became the school's director of development. He met with donors and asked them about their perceptions of the school—what they liked and what they did not like.

Said Leslie, "The need for a major campaign seemed obvious to everyone. The buildings on campus were aging and rickety. When I talked aboutan upcoming campaign, no one asked, 'Why are we doing this?' The climate was right."

In a campaign of this magnitude, whatever strengths or weaknesses an organization has will become more pronounced. In the case of Santa Fe Christian Schools, *Aspiring Beyond* allowed people to see how effective the school had truly been. The campaign provided a forum for underscoring the organization's mission, highlighting the school's achievements and soliciting major gifts.

With virtually 100 percent of its graduates moving on to college, and 90 percent of those heading to four-year schools, Santa Fe Christian Schools had followed through on its mission.

However, what was going on inside Santa Fe Christian Schools—proven success—was not evident in the buildings and grounds. The campus needed extensive capital improvements. But could a campaign to "fix up run-down buildings" produce the kind of groundswell created by this campaign? Not likely. Instead, SFCS raised the bar and energized prospective donors with the school's proven ability to achieve great things in the lives of its students.

The campaign took off because it was never about repairs or even new buildings. It was always about the mission to develop "tomorrow's Christian leaders." Every campus tour and prospect solicitation remained focused on this fact.

Few people other than Leslie and consultant Eric Staley originally expected million-dollar gifts, but they came in anyway. The level of giving for this campaign reflected strong support among donors for what Santa Fe Christian Schools had accomplished—not only what it had accomplished in the past, but what it was poised to do in the future.

Santa Fe Christian Schools could have raised money for a basic library and a computer lab, but the mission was not to develop good students; it was to develop tomorrow's leaders. Therefore, Santa Fe Christian Schools' goal was to create a library and computer lab commensurate with that mission.

Said Leslie, "Our library and technology center rivals anything around. One college student told us that students graduating from Santa Fe would find the college's tech program a step backward. Building this state-of-the-art library and tech center is a statement of the seriousness this school has regarding its commitment to excellence, without ever veering from its central Christian mission."

"Building this state-of-the-art library and tech center is a statement of the seriousness this school has regarding its commitment to excellence, without ever veering from its central Christian mission."

—CHUCK LESLIE
DIRECTOR OF DEVELOPMENT

One meaningful gift came from a volunteer whose grandchild had graduated from the school. Along with the $100,000 gift, he also brought a friend by the campus. After hearing about the campaign—and already familiar with the type of student graduating from the school—the friend offered an in-kind gift of a state-of-the-art phone system.

In-kind gifts were not uncommon. Donors were not compelled to give through obligation or coercion. Nor did they feel the school was in need of a bailout. The greatest motivating factor was seeing the school fulfill its mission. People who supported that mission were beyond willing—they were enthusiastic about giving to an organization making good on its promise.

Near the close of the campaign, Santa Fe Christian Schools received a third million-dollar gift. This one, given by the family of a new Santa Fe student, came as a complete surprise. What made the gift even more remarkable was that eight years prior, the father had been out of work. The caliber of students attending Santa Fe is what prompted him to give. He noticed this even before sending his child to the school. "It was our students—our mission—that prepped his generosity," said Leslie.

RESULTS:

The campaign resulted in substantial changes over the entire campus: major renovations and upgrades to virtually every building; a cutting-edge library and technology center; a science center; and additional classrooms. *Aspiring Beyond* also made a point of affirming the school's appreciation for its fine instructors. Ten percent of the total campaign, or $1 million, was set aside for a teachers' endowment. The campaign not only changed the look of the school, it changed the outlook. What it did not change was the mission.

CONSULTANT'S TIPS
CONSULTANT: R. ERIC STALEY, PhD

1. Never lose sight of the mission.
Do not dilute the organization's mission to make up for a shortage in money. Never diminish services or reduce standards just to keep a financial ship afloat. The mission is the message. Lowering the bar will never inspire greater giving from donors.

2. Raise the bar.
Motivate donors with enthusiasm, sound business practices, a compelling mission and positive results. Santa Fe Christian Schools went from a struggling nonprofit to a strongly funded superstar precisely because the leadership was willing to step out of their comfort zone, take hold of a greater vision than they had ever had before and remain focused on their mission.

3. Envision a dynamic future for the organization.
When it comes to creating a campaign to attract major gifts, it is better to envision a more inspiring future for the organization than it is to ask, "What can we do without?"

When financial challenges arise—a difficult economy, an increase in need, an unexpected hurdle—rather than shrink back, it is better for a nonprofit to keep an eye on the long-term mission and aspire beyond the short-term need.

Wentworth Military Academy & Junior College

Lexington, Missouri

CAMPAIGN NAME: "Securing the 21st Century"

CAMPAIGN TASK: To undergo major repairs and renovations throughout the campus; add new barracks; establish scholarship, faculty and maintenance endowments; wrap up construction on a fine arts center; and construct a new resource center.

ORIGINAL CAMPAIGN GOAL: $20 million

AMOUNT RAISED: $28 million

LENGTH OF CAMPAIGN: 29 months

SUPERINTENDENT & PRESIDENT: Major General John H. Little (U.S. Army, Ret.), Class of 1961

CAMPAIGN HIGHLIGHT:

This was a campaign of opportunities lost and opportunities found. The Wentworth leaders uncovered major gifts because they were willing to really listen to what potential donors had to say. Consultant Bud Cooper held 950 face-to-face meetings across the country, gathering prospect insights and opinions, as well as cultivating relationships in the process. The power of personal contact and the wisdom to listen with openness and respond with honesty not only turned this campaign into a monumental success, it managed to change hearts in the process.

MISSION:

To provide a foundation for the intellectual growth, leadership development and self-discipline essential to the men and women serving the nation as skilled leaders of moral character.

HISTORY:

After the death of his son in 1879, Stephen G. Wentworth established Wentworth Military Academy as a memorial in 1880.

THE CAMPAIGN FOR WENTWORTH MILITARY ACADEMY & JUNIOR COLLEGE:

The account of the Wentworth Military Academy campaign is really the story of a family. Said consultant Bud Cooper, "A school like this creates a bond that's not usually seen until college. For cadets, this was their home, 24 hours a day, seven days a week. This was their mother and father. They grew up here. This led to strong, positive feelings toward the school and each other. At Wentworth's 125th anniversary, the school will welcome alumni from around the world. They will travel thousands of miles to return to this place. That is how much Wentworth means to them."

"At Wentworth's 125th anniversary, the school will welcome alumni from around the world. They will travel thousands of miles to return to this place. That is how much Wentworth means to them."

—BUD COOPER, DMIN, CFRE
CONSULTANT

But it was this depth of emotion and feeling that also created a long-standing chasm between alumni and what they perceived as neglect from their alma mater (et pater). The very fact that they had spent their formative years at the knee of Wentworth Military Academy's instruction and had received so many influential, life-long lessons there made the silence between the Academy and the alumni especially awkward and hurtful.

When Cooper began his work with the Wentworth campaign, it quickly became clear that he would be the best person to reach out to the hundreds of potential prospects who first had to be located and then cultivated. But this would not be ordinary soil to cultivate—simply turned up and seeded with information about the campus. These were fields that had been left fallow for decades. Dryness and rocky relationships had to first be addressed with great sensitivity.

Since Cooper had no direct affiliation with the Academy other than as a consultant, he was able to enter these very delicate situations with impartiality, patience and understanding. Said Cooper, "I let them know I heard them. Without becoming defensive, I was able to sit there as an objective listener. These were people—many of whom had lost contact with the Academy."

Another hurdle was gathering names and numbers for alumni. Much of the information regarding alumni was outdated. The school was guilty of not seeking out lost contacts. For almost a year members of the steering committee made inquiries and even approached people about giving, but the process was hit and miss. Following a recommendation from the consultant, they took 7,000 names from the alumni list and applied technology to provide an overlay search of those names. By targeting graduates with the capacity to give major gifts, coupled with face-to-face meetings, the campaign started gaining momentum.

At first, prospective donors were hesitant. There had been no construction on campus in 38 years. It was important to encourage prospective donors to see the campus in a new light. "If you believe in something and have a passion, you can make things happen right before your very eyes," said Cooper.

"It's interesting," said General Little. "So many of our successful alumni, including myself, truly believe we owe something to Wentworth. The experience here in some way changed our lives. We feel an allegiance, almost a universal feeling of wanting to give something back." Yet, prior to this campaign, the alumni had been given very little encouragement to do so.

What the leadership team was able to accomplish was much more than attach donor dollars with an institution. Through *Securing the 21st Century*, they managed to take the negative feelings and emotions of prospective donors, turn things around and slowly walk people back to a place of reconnection and appreciation.

New buildings and barracks, refurbishments throughout the campus and the overall care of the grounds reflect more than the outcroppings of a financially successful campaign. They mirror the restoration of relationships. Lives reconnected with an institution that meant the world to them. What once needed repair is now renewed. What needed growth and vitality is now afresh with progress and expectancy. It is a new day for the campus, a new day for another generation of cadets and a new day for past graduates of the Wentworth family who, after a prolonged absence, have finally come home.

> *"So many of our successful alumni, including myself, truly believe we owe something to Wentworth. The experience here in some way changed our lives."*
>
> —MAJOR GENERAL JOHN H. LITTLE, PRESIDENT

RESULTS:

Wentworth has dramatically expanded the personal information in its donor base and significantly increased its potential for receiving gifts. Improvements to campus barracks produced other positives for Wentworth. With new barracks in place, recruitment is easier. In addition to the many capital improvements, scholarships are also up, and a faculty endowment will help ensure that Wentworth can continue to attract and retain the very best instructors. Restoration of historically registered buildings, including the renovation of the Chapel and the remodeling of a century-old administrative building to include the new fine arts facility, demonstrates Wentworth's respect for the past. Restoration of alumni relationships confirms the school's commitment to the present and future of Wentworth Military Academy.

Consultant's Tips

Consultant: H. Layton (Bud) Cooper, DMin, CFRE

Major gifts flow from major relationships. Build a relationship and you build the potential for greater gifts in the future.

1. Attention.
Don't let the mistakes of the past keep your organization from turning things around.

2. At ease.
Refuse to take offense when prospective donors tell you what they think.

3. Present arms.
Consider it a privilege to hear the donor's point of view, even if it reflects negatively on the organization.

4. Forward, march.
Use this invaluable information to enlighten and improve the organization.

Frustration often reflects strong feelings. If donors are passionate, it probably means they care deeply about the organization. Allow this passion to be channeled from frustration to expression to appreciation. You can turn things around if you are willing to listen past what donors say to hear what they mean.

Truman Medical Centers

Kansas City, Missouri

CAMPAIGN NAME: "Realize the Vision"

CAMPAIGN TASK: Renovations and equipment for intensive care additions, critical care surgery, and labor and delivery wings; programmatic patient care; and physician-chaired positions.

ORIGINAL CAMPAIGN GOAL: $20 million

AMOUNT RAISED: $20.5 million

LENGTH OF CAMPAIGN: 36 months

PRESIDENT/CEO: John Bluford

DIRECTOR OF DEVELOPMENT: Mark Litzler

CAMPAIGN HIGHLIGHT:

Peripheral issues surrounding an organization can affect and influence a campaign. While these situations—sometimes positive, sometimes negative—are impossible to ignore completely, fundraisers must, nonetheless, remain focused. Throughout the campaign, Truman Medical Centers experienced several changes in administration. Turnovers in CEOs, policies and related public perceptions could have been a huge distraction to the campaign. Instead, the leadership of Truman Medical Centers chose to stay attentive to the task at hand.

MISSION:

To provide accessible, state-of-the-art health care to the community.

HISTORY:

The Truman Medical Centers began in 1870 in a small, frame building two blocks outside the city limits. Truman Medical Center on Hospital Hill was the city's first public health facility. The Truman Medical Centers corporation acquired Truman Medical Center East in 1973. The Truman Medical Center (TMC) Charitable Foundation was formed in 1979 to develop and oversee charitable support for the hospital system.

THE CAMPAIGN FOR TRUMAN MEDICAL CENTERS:

From a single building more than 130 years ago to a major medical complex today, the Truman Medical Centers has exemplified what it means to care about others. The hospital has a long tradition of providing medical attention to patients regardless of their ability to pay. It is the largest health-care provider—a safety net—for the medically indigent population of Kansas City and Jackson County, Missouri.

Truman Medical Center on Hospital Hill and Truman East share complementary missions of care and education. Both hospitals provide patients with medical attention, while serving as teaching hospitals for the University of Missouri—Kansas City School of Medicine. A multimillion-dollar campaign was necessary for the hospital to meet growing needs both in dispensing medical care and in fulfilling its role as a teaching hospital.

> *"The hospital had fostered years of goodwill. This capital campaign was really the first time we had asked for money in a big way."*
>
> —MARK LITZLER
> DIRECTOR OF DEVELOPMENT

"We had a little concern about the capacity of this community to support a $20 million campaign. Truman had never undertaken a fundraising venture in this fashion before," said Ned Holland, Truman Medical Centers board member for 26 years and president of the Charitable Medical Foundation.

"It was steady work for everyone over the two-year period," said Director of Development Mark Litzler. "Of course Ned Holland was there from the beginning, but we had some unusual public relations issues—four CEOs in three years. Our consultant helped us navigate this terrain and stay on track."

Counsel Bob Hartsook explained, "As a safety-net institution they really needed to stay focused on the century of good they had achieved in Kansas City. Changes in top management aside, it was the mission of Truman Medical Centers that mattered most."

"The hospital had fostered years of goodwill. This capital campaign was really the first time we had asked for money in a big way," said Litzler. As it turned out, the community also responded in a big way.

Staying focused was not always easy, but it was imperative. One of the biggest reasons campaigns stall is because members of the leadership team become preoccupied with ancillary issues. When they turn their gaze from the organization's mission and purpose, they start to falter. Poor press, new management, changes in the economy—none of these are the ultimate reasons why donors choose to give. They give because they want to see people helped in meaningful and life-impacting ways. This is exactly what Truman Medical Centers does every day.

In order to provide continuing care for patients with little to no ability to pay, it was essential for Truman Medical Centers' fundraisers to maintain an emotional distance from day-to-day turns of events in the organization. They were not oblivious to the changes, but they did not let them become a focal point or a drain on time and energy.

"When we started, we didn't even *know* what we didn't know about fundraising. We learned a great deal through the process. The money raised is tremendous for Truman Medical Centers, but better still is the increased profile and philanthropic capacity we now have in the community," offered Holland.

Litzler agreed that illuminating TMC's mission—particularly that of providing state-of-the-art care to indigent people in the community—was vital not only to the community but to the campaign.

"The hospital is in better shape today because of the campaign—and not just financially. Even during times of transition within the organization we succeeded in reaching the $20 million mark. Most nonprofits can look to one CEO to help close some significant gifts. Our strength was a clear mission that the community could understand, believe in and support," said Litzler.

> *"The hospital is in better shape today because of the campaign—and not just financially."*
>
> —MARK LITZLER
> DIRECTOR OF DEVELOPMENT

RESULTS:

Realize the Vision raised support to endow several new chairs: The Schutte Chair in Women's Health, The Sosland Chair in Trauma Services, and The Williams Chair in Community and Family Medicine. These chaired positions help attract physicians of national stature to the hospital center. Additions to intensive care, critical care surgery, and labor and delivery, as well as program enhancements to patient care, were all benefits of *Realize the Vision*.

CONSULTANT'S TIPS

CONSULTANT: ROBERT F. HARTSOOK, JD, EdD

Just as Truman Medical Centers held fast to its mission, every organization should keep an eye on the destination rather than become distracted by the changing landscape of organizational politics. To do so:

1. **Build a case.**
   Develop a strong and compelling case for support highlighting the organization's ultimate mission.

2. **Reinforce the mission.**
   Make sure everyone involved—staff, board members and volunteers—is familiar with the case and the accomplishments of the organization.

3. **Stick to business.**
   Do not get caught up in the highs and lows of the organization—media attention, water-cooler gossip, changing of the guards.

4. **Deliver the message.**
   Stay committed to telling the organization's story directly and effectively to prospective donors.

The National Dance Institute—New Mexico

Santa Fe, New Mexico

CAMPAIGN NAME: "Making the Move"

CAMPAIGN TASK: To build a new facility for offices, rehearsals and productions; and to create an endowment for the future.

ORIGINAL CAMPAIGN GOAL: $7 million

AMOUNT RAISED: $7.34 million

LENGTH OF CAMPAIGN: 22 months

ARTISTIC DIRECTOR: Catherine Oppenheimer

MANAGING DIRECTOR: Gemtria St. Clair

DIRECTOR OF DEVELOPMENT: Kelley Barnes

Campaign Highlight:

Over the years, National Dance Institute—New Mexico (NDI-NM) performances have earned a reputation for exceeding expectations, bringing audiences to their feet and moving the children who participate in these rigorous dance programs from apathy to passion, from vulnerability to strength and from unseen student to star-studded hero. It is something one must see to appreciate fully. It takes the power of the performance to really understand what this organization accomplishes in the lives of children. NDI-NM successfully used the campaign itself as a conduit of cultivation and a tool for solicitation.

Mission:

The National Dance Institute—New Mexico was founded with the knowledge that the arts have a unique power to engage and motivate children. The purpose of the distinctive dance programs is to help children develop discipline, a standard of excellence and a belief in themselves that will carry over into all aspects of their lives.

History:

As a dancer with the New York City Ballet, Jacques d'Amboise developed the National Dance Institute in 1976. Dance had changed the course of his life, turning him away from the streets toward a successful career. He received a MacArthur Fellowship in 1990 that led him and his wife to New Mexico. There they introduced the National Dance Institute to several Santa Fe elementary public schools. In 1994, Catherine Oppenheimer, a dancer with the New York City Ballet and the Twyla Tharp Dance Company, relocated to help establish the NDI-NM. A year later, the Institute received nonprofit status. Oppenheimer's home served as headquarters until 1998, when NDI-NM relocated to Santa Fe's historic "Pink Church."

THE CAMPAIGN FOR THE NATIONAL DANCE INSTITUTE—NEW MEXICO:

NDI-NM had never attempted a campaign anywhere near this size. It was a big goal, but there was no question about the importance of the mission or the amazing results the organization had already achieved in the lives of thousands of children.

Since no child is excluded from the NDI-NM program, the able-bodied and children with disabilities fill the stage and join in the dance. Simply telling a donor what NDI-NM does is not enough. Said consultant Susan Thomas, "It is a tactile experience. It's something the donor must see, smell, hear and touch." It takes more creativity, organization and, at times, friendly persuasion to get donors to an event rather than carrying pictures and papers to a solicitation visit, but for NDI-NM it was time well spent.

> *"It is a tactile experience. It's something the donor must see, smell, hear and touch."*
>
> —SUSAN THOMAS, CFRE
> CONSULTANT

More than half of the children served by NDI-NM live below the poverty line. Dance is a way to forget about problems just outside the door. But for NDI-NM staff and instructors, dance serves only as a medium. The message is that hard work, discipline and an uncompromising standard of excellence will produce confidence, increase abilities and open doors for a brighter future.

Young dancers participating in the NDI-NM program experience marked improvements in reading, language arts, spelling, math, social studies and conduct. Parents and teachers offer example after example of children who have been positively changed through their involvement with the program.

Yet, even with these impressive outcomes, nothing on paper can compete with the sparkling eyes, quick steps, bright smiles and unbridled joy that flows from the dancers during a final performance. The stage comes alive with hundreds of children bursting with life and sound and rhythm.

From the beginning of the campaign, everyone understood that any solicitation of a gift would be greatly diminished if the donor had not seen NDI-NM in action. "Seeing is believing," said Medora Jennings, board president at the time of the campaign. "The dedication of the instructors, the concentration on the faces of these children—it all shows through as they're performing. We knew if we could get a prospective donor to one of our dances—or take them to a class—then we had them."

NDI-NM used several means of cultivation—connecting donors to the organization both intellectually and emotionally. One method was "Take a Friend to Class." A board member would invite friends to watch the children practice. This was often a very effective means for building interest in the organization.

But what was even more helpful was if a board member invited several friends at once, with a meal or refreshments following. In this way, conversation could naturally follow, creating a buzz of new enthusiasm for the NDI-NM building project. It connected more "friends" with the program— friends who knew others who might be interested in showing their support.

"Hard Hat Tours" also proved to be a very popular means for donor cultivation. As the facility began to take shape, prospects donned hard hats and took tours of what would soon become a building filled with music and movement. Curiosity helped persuade many visitors to take a look. Said Thomas, "People wanted to see how the building was shaping up. It was so much better than looking at renderings and words on paper." Throughout the tour, prospects heard about the demonstrative results NDI-NM had achieved in the lives of children. Often, curiosity led to a greater level of interest in the campaign.

A community Dance-a-Thon also turned out to be a great cultivation tool. Proceeds from the actual event were small by comparison with leadership gifts, but the event helped increase campaign visibility and drew in 400 new gifts.

Receptions, cocktail parties and small group dinners, while more traditional, were equally successful methods used for cultivating donors. The conversation always came back to what a wonderful impact NDI-NM was having on so many children—and how important it was for the Institute to reach out to more public schools, to serve even more children. "You're never raising money for a building," said Thomas. "You're raising money for what goes on inside the building."

> *"The dedication of the instructors, the concentration on the faces of these children—it all shows through as they're performing. We knew if we could get a prospective donor to one of our dances—or take them to a class—then we had them."*
>
> —Medora Jennings
> Former Board President

In less than two years, NDI-NM reached and surpassed its goal of $7 million. Added Thomas, "The success they achieved was really a result of the time and energy put into cultivating donors."

Results:

Offering tours and inviting people to experience the impact of the organization worked wonders for this campaign. Not only is NDI-NM settled into its new 31,000-square-foot facility, but opening ceremonies included a visit from First Lady Laura Bush, acknowledging the organization's efforts as, "… a great example of what can happen when children are inspired to share their gifts with the world." The campaign also established a strong endowment to ensure that thousands more children can participate in this life-changing program for many years to come.

CONSULTANT'S TIPS

CONSULTANTS: SUSAN DUNCAN THOMAS, CFRE
& MADELYN (MANDY) PONS

The best cultivation does not have to take place in a posh restaurant, out on the links or even in a prospect's living room. The goal of cultivation is to connect the donor with the organization both intellectually and emotionally.

1. Open the doors.
Don't just talk about what the organization accomplishes. Let the campaign act as its own vehicle for cultivation.

2. Pack 'em in.
Whenever appropriate, invite donors into the life of the organization and allow them to observe the positive outcomes of the mission firsthand.

3. Put on a show.
Don't keep cultivation solely between the development personnel and the donor. Allow those who benefit from the mission to help cultivate support for the organization.

When donors ask what the organization is achieving, don't be satisfied with just talking about it. Respond with an invitation, "Let us show you!"

CHAPTER TWO

TAKE IT ONE DAY AT A TIME

*"You can learn a lot
by watching."*

—*Yogi Berra*

American Red Cross, Midway-Kansas Chapter

Wichita, Kansas

CAMPAIGN NAME: "Together We Can Save a Life"

CAMPAIGN TASK: To purchase and renovate a larger building to replace the 24-year-old Chapter location. The existing facility had become too small to meet the community's needs and accommodate the services needed. Adding space was not feasible.

ORIGINAL CAMPAIGN GOAL: $5.9 million

AMOUNT RAISED: $6.1 million

LENGTH OF CAMPAIGN: 24 months

EXECUTIVE DIRECTOR: Beverly Morlan

DIRECTOR OF DEVELOPMENT: Linda Wright

CAMPAIGN HIGHLIGHT:

Fundraising can be a roller coaster ride. No matter how fast or slow, up or down the campaign goes, hold on. Twists and turns are inevitable, but staying on track is imperative. It is important not to get too excited when things are going well or too down when things are not turning out as planned. The Midway-Kansas Chapter had a natural disposition to take this advice to heart and manage the cyclical emotions of a campaign.

MISSION:

To provide relief to victims of disasters and help people prevent, prepare for and respond to emergencies. It does this through services that are consistent with its congressional charter and the fundamental principles of the International Red Cross movement.

HISTORY:

The International Red Cross and Red Crescent Movement was created in Geneva, Switzerland in 1863 to provide non-partisan care to the wounded and sick in times of war. The Midway-Kansas Chapter of the American Red Cross was founded in 1915.

THE CAMPAIGN FOR AMERICAN RED CROSS, MIDWAY-KANSAS CHAPTER:

"The executive director, director of development and co-chairs for this campaign were masterful at not letting themselves get too high or too low. They didn't agonize over disappointments or get caught up too long in the excitement of a big gift," said consultant Robert Swanson.

Together We Can Save a Life was already in progress during the September 11 attacks. Other campaign leaders might have been tempted to quit. In contrast, the Midway-Kansas Chapter recognized the horrific events of 9/11 as evidence of the need to press through. The organization needed to secure a building and fund programs to adequately serve the city of Wichita—whatever the future might hold.

Said Executive Director Bev Morlan, "I told my staff, the board and volunteers, 'We can stop in the middle of this campaign, but our clients need us now more than ever. A sagging economy and 9/11 are not reasons to stop this campaign. Those factors are even more reason to push forward.'"

> *"I told my staff, the board and volunteers, 'We can stop in the middle of this campaign, but our clients need us now more than ever. A sagging economy and 9/11 are not reasons to stop this campaign. Those factors are even more reason to push forward.'"*
>
> —BEV MORLAN
> EXECUTIVE DIRECTOR

Campaign Co-Chair Barry West echoed her sentiments, "We could have lowered the goal or put the campaign on hiatus, but what would that accomplish? The organization needed this campaign to meet real needs of real people in our area."

Naturally, there were setbacks as well as exciting moments, but the staff and campaign volunteers continued to take them all in stride and remained focused on the work of the campaign. "Each month, we reviewed what had been accomplished or not accomplished, and then outlined the next month's action items and went forward," said West.

"We certainly had some disappointments along the way," admitted former Board President Sue Pearce. Added Morlan, "Even when we had our down moments, though, we never felt alone or thought we would fail." A close and congenial relationship bonded the campaign team. It helped keep emotions stable and bolster a spirit of encouragement during the tough times and celebration during the good times.

Traditionally, more people say no than say yes. Recognizing that on the front end helps to manage expectations and emotions. When something great happens, don't go off the charts. When you face a challenge, don't give in to despair.

The Midway-Kansas Chapter had the opportunity to succumb to both extremes—positive distraction and negative despair. The aftermath of 9/11 created a very difficult financial climate for Wichita. One of the city's key industries—aviation—was particularly hard hit by the attacks. Rather than crumble under the weight of discouragement, the organization redoubled its strategy to diversify the donor prospect pool.

In contrast, when a surprise gift of $500,000 arrived, the leadership team resisted the temptation to let the excitement knock them off course. Along with his gift, the donor enclosed letters he had written to his mother during World War II. They were replete with references about the care and compassion he received from the Red Cross following his combat injuries. While this represented a very uplifting and substantial gift, the campaign team knew better than to overcelebrate the windfall or become distracted from the task at hand.

The Midway-Kansas Chapter was a perfect example of how to maintain an even keel throughout a campaign. Whenever a challenge arose, they faced it with a "let's-go-get-it-done" attitude. Whenever a solicitation went well or a grant was accepted, they used that energy and momentum to push forward.

> *"Our consultant always reminded us that the campaign was about more than the money. Of course, we had to raise the money, but it was really about engaging more people in this great organization."*
>
> —MARC COLBY
> CAMPAIGN CO-CHAIR

Said Campaign Co-Chair Marc Colby, "Our consultant always reminded us that the campaign was about more than the money. Of course, we had to raise the money, but it was really about engaging more people in this great organization. Obviously, sometimes there were reasons to think we might fail—the economy, the sheer magnitude of the campaign goal. But in the end, it wasn't about a campaign and it wasn't about us; it was about saving lives."

RESULTS:

The vacant building they purchased was perfect for the Chapter's needs. Said Board President Susan Franz Koslowsky, "It had visibility, lots of parking, easy access and space to grow." Newly renovated, the building gives the organization much needed square footage for blood services as well as emergency social services, disaster relief programs and a better emergency-response staging area. Parking, which had become a big dilemma at the former location, is no longer a problem. "Every year more than 70,000 people are served by this Chapter," said Colby. "Now we are in a much better position to serve people and save lives."

CONSULTANT'S TIPS

CONSULTANT: ROBERT G. SWANSON

Never let emotions get the best of you during a campaign. In fundraising, as in life, discipline and consistency will reap the greatest rewards.

1. Take it one day at a time.

…Or at least a month at a time. Stay focused on a short list of tasks rather than looking at the campaign as the two- or three-year adventure it will ultimately be.

2. Break it into little bites.

Think in terms of the next half-million dollars rather than the $6 million total. "Eat that elephant a bite at a time."

3. Celebrate victories (but not for too long).

It is natural to be excited about a $500,000 gift, but let the celebration serve as a motivation to get back out there and raise more money.

4. Commiserate over disappointments (but not for too long).

Acknowledge disappointments, but quickly move right back to the job at hand. The sooner you are back making calls, meeting people and getting the organization's story out there, the sooner you will have reason to celebrate once again.

Tulsa Boys' Home

Sand Springs, Oklahoma

CAMPAIGN NAME: "Vision 2000"

CAMPAIGN TASK: To undergo major campus renovations and additions: new cottages, training
and education center, sports complex, dining
hall and upgrades throughout the campus.

ORIGINAL CAMPAIGN GOAL: $3.7 million

AMOUNT RAISED: $3.7 million, plus a Donald W.
Reynolds Foundation grant of $11.6 million

LENGTH OF CAMPAIGN: 18 months

EXECUTIVE DIRECTOR: Gregory T. Conway

Campaign Highlight:

The campaign, *Vision 2000*, turned a committed campus into a nationally recognized, state-of-the-art facility. The incredible changes happening at Tulsa Boys' Home were too momentous to simply discuss with donors. They had to be seen. By bringing donors onto the campus and involving them in the life of the institution, *Vision 2000* managed to raise more than funds; it raised new friends.

Mission:

To provide the highest quality residential care for boys and young men needing placement outside their home, for the purpose of developing well-adjusted, responsible adults and strengthening the family.

History:

Founded in 1918 by the Rotary Club and First Presbyterian Church, Tulsa Boys' Home began in downtown Tulsa providing shelter and meals for orphans or boys who had left home. Today Tulsa Boys' Home serves as a residential treatment facility for boys, ages 13 through 18, with serious emotional or behavioral problems who require temporary placement outside the home.

The Campaign for Tulsa Boys' Home:

It is impossible to understand the impact of Tulsa Boys' Home without hearing about boys whose lives have been changed by the organization. Take David, for example. Before arriving at Tulsa Boys' Home, he was at risk of becoming just one more statistic.

"When I first heard about Tulsa Boys' Home from a juvenile probation officer I thought it was just a place for hard-core delinquents," said David. "I soon realized it was a place where I could get help. They taught me the skills I needed to get my life back on track." After graduating from high school and working two jobs, David took college entrance exams and has every hope of pursuing a career in law enforcement.

> *"Even before I agreed to serve as executive director, I knew this organization had the history, tradition, mission and commitment to achieve great things."*
>
> —Gregg Conway
> Executive Director

What Tulsa Boys' Home has been able to achieve in the lives of boys is difficult to convey in a brochure or newsletter. It became evident that donors who were invited to see the campus firsthand became noticeably more involved in the success of the campaign as well as the mission of the Home.

"Even before I agreed to serve as executive director," said Gregg Conway, "I knew this organization had the history, tradition, mission and commitment to achieve great things. One of my goals from the very beginning was to undertake a capital campaign to position Tulsa Boys' Home as a world-class leader in our field. I wanted to see it turned into a state-of-the-art facility for troubled boys—nothing less."

Conway's passion caught fire. Board members began by giving financially to the campaign. Then they started contacting friends and associates who might also be interested in Tulsa Boys' Home. Through these contacts and others, *Vision 2000* not only generated millions of dollars for the institution but attracted strong new donor relationships.

"One thing Bob [Hartsook] mentioned to us early on was that we could benefit from some public relations work," Conway said. "The community knew we were here, but they were not sure of our mission and they certainly didn't know where we were headed in the next century. In combination with the campaign, we began putting our story out to the community, telling people exactly what we did and what we planned to achieve in the future."

Getting that story out included bringing prospects and donors to see the campus in action. Nothing could convey the value of the institution or the necessity of the campaign like a tour of the grounds and facilities. Said consultant Bob Hartsook, "The Boys' Home is located a good 20 to 30 minutes outside of Tulsa. Getting prospects and previous donors to visit is not the easiest thing to do logistically. Having donors see the progress being made on the campus and interact with the boys demonstrates the impact of Tulsa Boys' Home more than any phone call or written description could hope to do." The benefit of getting donors to see the work of an organization firsthand far outweighs the extra effort.

One donor, who had given smaller gifts in the past, was invited to the campus for a tour. While on tour, he was able to observe the boys going through their daily activities. He saw their name badges with designations—Novice, Page, Squire, Knight, and the most coveted rank, Order of the Lions. He was told that by moving up the ranks—achieving specific goals and objectives—boys gained more autonomy and earned the privilege of entering the "Lions' Den" where they could watch movies, play video games and hang out with other Lions.

Seeing these youthful faces impacted this donor in a profound way. He realized that these were normal boys—just like his own nephew or the neighbor down the street. But he understood that it was through excruciatingly painful circumstances that these young men had arrived at Tulsa Boys' Home. The effect of seeing them interact in the cafeteria, hearing their laughter and watching them play ball in the gymnasium provided an emotional connection for this man that a solicitation letter or visit could never produce. Even without being asked, he wrote out a check for $5,000 and was glad to do it.

> *"The incredible publicity and positive response from the community heightened the Home's visibility and greatly enhanced our influence."*
>
> —GREGG CONWAY
> EXECUTIVE DIRECTOR

Many such visits and tours added up to significant financial support and stronger donor relationships. In addition, an $11.6 million grant from the Donald W. Reynolds Foundation—above the campaign goal of $3.7 million—turned the original master plan (to be phased in over time) into a blueprint for immediate action.

"The incredible publicity and positive response from the community heightened the Home's visibility and greatly enhanced our influence," said Conway. "I can't go anywhere anymore without someone saying, 'Hey, you're with Tulsa Boys' Home, right? Heard what you're doing out there. Great job!' It's had a real impact beyond the major changes on campus."

With such dramatic changes to the campus, it has been important for donors to see the impact of the campaign and the boys who benefit. Offered a Tulsa Boys' Home staff member, "Donors who visit the facility always leave with a greater connection to the Home. They don't just think in terms of giving money to the organization. They feel a part of who we are and what we do."

RESULTS:

The new Donald W. Reynolds Training Center allows Tulsa Boys' Home to host a number of seminars and events on campus. New cottages, a sports complex and pool, full-court gymnasium, and biking and fitness trail set a new standard for residential treatment facilities. Said Conway, "Everything that isn't new will receive a major facelift." *Vision 2000* has helped create a state-of-the-art facility that will serve as a national model for other organizations.

CONSULTANT'S TIPS
CONSULTANT: ROBERT F. HARTSOOK, JD, EDD

It is not always enough to tell major prospective donors about the organization. It is even more important to give them an insider's perspective.

1. Extend an invitation.
Invite prospective donors to take a tour of the organization.

2. Plan ahead.
Coordinate the visit to coincide with special events.

3. Build trust.
Give the prospective donor a feeling of being on the inside of the organization.

4. Revisit the idea.
Bring donors back for a visit—after a gift has been secured—to see the impact their gifts have made.

Special Olympics Kansas

Mission, Kansas

CAMPAIGN NAME: "Together We Win"

CAMPAIGN TASK: To purchase and renovate a building, create a maintenance fund for the facility, add a staff person to oversee operations, and support the technological needs of the organization and its athletes.

ORIGINAL CAMPAIGN GOAL: $1.35 million

AMOUNT RAISED: $1.35 million plus

LENGTH OF CAMPAIGN: 20 months

EXECUTIVE DIRECTOR: Chris Hahn

DIRECTOR OF DEVELOPMENT: Adrian DeWendt

CAMPAIGN HIGHLIGHT:

Why is it that fundraising stories with the greatest sticki-ness—memorability—are least representative of solid strate-gies? No one can plan for an "out-of-the-blue" gift. In direct contrast to the one-in-a-million long-shot odds of an unso-licited gift, it is important for nonprofits to understand that it is always the people closest to the organization who will make the greatest difference. Major gifts will virtually all come—either directly or indirectly—from the organization's most ardent supporters.

MISSION:

To provide year-round sports training and athletic competi-tion in a variety of Olympic-type sports for individuals with mental retardation by giving them continuing opportunities to develop physical fitness, demonstrate courage, experi-ence joy and participate in a sharing of gifts, skills and friendship with their families, other Special Olympics ath-letes and the community.

HISTORY:

Special Olympics started in 1968. Eunice Kennedy Shriver organized the First International Special Olympics Games at Soldier Field, Chicago, Illinois, USA. Mrs. Shriver had started a day camp in the early 1960s for people with mental retardation. Special Olympics Kansas (SOK) began in 1970. Today it includes more than 100 local programs and teams across the state.

THE CAMPAIGN FOR SPECIAL OLYMPICS KANSAS:

The Athlete Oath, "Let me win, but if I cannot win, let me be brave in the attempt," typifies the courageous spirit of Special Olympics and the people who make the organization work.

Said board member John Meara, "It's rare to find a board that feels so passionately about what it is doing. Being involved with Special Olympics is one of the most rewarding experiences I've ever had in civic or charitable work. Everyone contributes their time out of the love of being with Special Olympians."

Due to SOK's tremendous growth and expansion over the past quarter century, the organization had outgrown its state corporate office and training facility. They really needed a new education and program center to address existing and future demands for services.

> "It's rare to find a board that feels so passionately about what it is doing. Being involved with Special Olympics is one of the most rewarding experiences I've ever had in civic or charitable work."
>
> —JOHN MEARA
> BOARD MEMBER

An initial obstacle to the campaign was actually the result of an oxymoron-esque "wonderful problem." An excellent find of an existing facility prompted SOK to purchase its new building in advance of the campaign kick off. SOK was then forced to explain to donors why the organization needed facility monies.

As SOK found out, it is always preferable to initiate a campaign for the purchase or construction of a building rather than buy it and then go raise money to fund it. Fortunately, this was a challenge they managed to overcome.

Said Dale Chaffin, campaign committee chairman and board member, "Our consultant Murray Blackwelder helped us make a case to our constituency. We learned through the campaign process how things needed to be executed in an organized and scientific manner."

Another lesson came early in the campaign. "Everyone thinks it's someone new and unknown who will ride in with a big gift and save the day. The truth is, it's always the people closest to you that make the difference in a campaign," said Blackwelder.

To prove his point, Blackwelder made sure that the leadership team was constantly discussing prospect possibilities and nailing down who would be the best choice for cultivating and securing a particular gift.

Said Blackwelder, "Eighty to 90 percent of the time, someone close to the organization closes the deal on a major gift." Nonprofits are always toying with the thought that, "If we send a letter to everyone in the state, maybe a big gift will come in." Instead, board-training sessions were used to keep everyone focused on the goal in terms of the number of gifts needed over $150,000 and those needed between $25,000 and $100,000. From there, Blackwelder asked the board and volunteers to consider the people they knew who might fill those spots.

In the end, there were some surprises for SOK—as there are in any campaign that does the necessary homework and conducts the proper solicitations. The organization anticipated a single gift above $150,000, with the majority of gifts coming in between $25,000 and $99,000. As it turned out, three gifts over $150,000 surfaced with an additional two gifts over $100,000, and five in the $50,000 to $99,000 range.

When challenged to consider their own contacts as potential major donors, board members became extremely adept at identifying good prospects. Board member Dave Lindstrom, a Burger King franchise owner and former Kansas City Chiefs player, was instrumental in getting SOK a lead gift of more than $150,000.

Another valued gift arrived after an honorary chairperson connected a prospective donor with the organization's mission. A board member/stockbroker had a client who was talking about making a legacy gift to an organization on his and his wife's behalf. Once the board member understood what the couple was interested in doing, he was able to introduce them to the great work of Special Olympics Kansas and invite them to make a gift to the campaign. They committed $500,000.

"Everyone thinks it's someone new and unknown who will ride in with a big gift and save the day. The truth is, it's always the people closest to you that make the difference in a campaign."

—MURRAY BLACKWELDER
CONSULTANT

Yes, someone could have shown up on a white horse, dropped a multimillion-dollar gift and ridden off into the sunset in quiet anonymity. On the other hand, it was better for SOK in the long run to build a broader base of friends who could be naturally connected to the organization and cultivated for a major gift. They recognized that the people closest to the organization end up making the biggest difference—either directly or through their association.

RESULTS:

Special Olympics Kansas now has a long-term financial future—a headquarters owned outright, an endowment that will cover maintenance expenses, new paid area directors with some of these positions endowed and stellar, up-to-date technology for its offices. Said Chris Hahn, SOK's president and CEO, in understated fashion, "It's a wonderful position to be in."

CONSULTANT'S TIPS

CONSULTANT: MURRAY BLACKWELDER

Fundraising is not first cousin to the Lottery. They are not even related. Do not look at fundraising opportunities as lightening-bolt events or unexplained phenomena.

1. **Remember** that major gifts will come from the people closest to the organization—either directly or through association.

2. **Educate board members, staff and volunteers** that major gifts will come from the people closest to the organization—either directly or through association.

(Beginning to see a theme?)

3. **Be grateful** if an unexplained appearance of money arises during a campaign, but don't hold your breath for another sighting.

Major gifts are not miraculous in nature. They are received as a result of diligent research, tireless cultivation and deliberate asking.

Boone County Empowerment Board

Boone, Iowa

CAMPAIGN NAME: "Family Resource Center…
Building for Generations"

CAMPAIGN TASK: To build an 18,000-square-foot
facility for the newly developed Boone Family
Resource Center. The Family Resource Center
serves as a central location for individual and
family-centered services, including early
childhood education programs, child-care and
adult day services.

ORIGINAL CAMPAIGN GOAL: $2.1 million

AMOUNT RAISED: $2.5 million

LENGTH OF CAMPAIGN: 24 months

EMPOWERMENT COORDINATOR AND DIRECTOR OF
DEVELOPMENT: Sara Behn

CAMPAIGN HIGHLIGHT:

Major gift fundraising is a new concept for many nonprofit organizations and their volunteers. Such was the case for the Empowerment Board Planning Committee and their volunteers. For some, the idea of approaching a prospective donor was unsettling. So getting these same volunteers to ask for a specific, large gift amount took some effort, much ongoing encouragement and a whole new way of thinking about philanthropy.

MISSION:

To provide outreach to families in the Boone County Empowerment Area; to improve access to opportunities, resources and supports needed to build strong healthy families; to eliminate barriers to families seeking services; to create and sustain a unified system of education, health and social services; and to support families in meeting their children's emotional, physical and social needs.

HISTORY:

The Empowerment program was mandated by the Iowa State Legislature to provide services to Iowa families with children from birth through five years of age. Boone County received its Empowerment designation in 1998. The Boone County Empowerment Board receives broad community support from private citizens, schools, child-care providers, the Department of Human Services, health-care providers, churches, the Chamber of Commerce and various human-service providers.

THE CAMPAIGN FOR BOONE COUNTY EMPOWERMENT BOARD:

Said consultant Jean Kresse, "It was exciting to be involved with an organization that had never raised private funds in the past. We took a one-person office whose main responsibility was overseeing contracted services for the residents of Boone County and created a full-fledged development department."

The Family Resource Center Planning Committee was formed by the Boone County Empowerment Board to investigate the possibilities of creating a centralized facility to house the new and expanded programs. Three subcommittees were formed to research and analyze the best choices for location, programming and financial issues related to a new facility. The members of the committee were focused, diligent and committed. They were not, however, entirely comfortable soliciting large gifts.

"There was a significant learning curve for us with this campaign. Many of our volunteers were uncomfortable with the idea of asking for a specific gift amount."

—SARA BEHN
EMPOWERMENT COORDINATOR
& DIRECTOR OF DEVELOPMENT

Said Sara Behn, who serves as both empowerment coordinator and director of development, "There was a significant learning curve for us with this campaign. Many of our volunteers were uncomfortable with the idea of asking for a specific gift amount."

Some wonderful gifts and matching opportunities helped motivate volunteers to make the most effective solicitations possible. The lead gift, a private donation of $100,000, came anonymously from a Boone County couple. Later on, this same couple gave another challenge gift to the community, matching every dollar raised for an additional gift of $150,000.

An Iowa Department of Economic Development Community Development Block Grant of $600,000, with the City of Boone as applicant, gave the campaign greater momentum.

The City of Boone agreed to serve as the Center's owner/operator and committed $500,000 in seed funds through the Garvey Trust Fund. In addition, the City committed a challenge grant to the community, doubling every dollar raised privately up to $400,000.

With such a show of support, volunteers understood how important it was to solicit gifts—not only to meet the goal, but to match generous public and private challenge gifts. However, asking for a specific amount was still a leap for some volunteers. They were concerned they might come across as presumptuous or pushy.

Offered Behn, "Solicitation training sessions and actual experiences encouraged our volunteers and got them thinking in new ways. Although it was difficult for some of them to get to a new place of asking, many did."

The committee soon learned that their concerns were actually the opposite of real-life solicitation experiences. Once prospective donors had been properly identified as having both a capacity to give and an adequate level of interest in the organization's mission, being asked for a specific gift was appreciated, not resented.

Donors do not want to disappoint, nor do they want to fall short of the organization's needs or expectations for a certain level of giving. But how can they possibly know how much that is unless they are asked for a specific dollar amount? "We were told, 'The worst thing that can happen is for the donor to say no or to give an amount less than what you have asked.' If you go in expecting a gift of $1,000 and you don't ask for that amount, you will probably walk out with a check for $100. You will be disappointed and the donor won't have a chance to meet your expectations," said Behn.

One donor, when asked for more than expected, took a slight gasp of air and said, "I'm surprised you think I have assets to make that large of a gift." If anything, the donor took the stretch amount as a compliment that she was held in such high financial esteem. Not only did she make the gift, she exceeded the ask.

Through ongoing support and encouragement, volunteers became familiar with the solicitation process. They began to notice for themselves that whenever they failed to ask for a specific amount, they returned with a smaller gift than expected. Whenever they were willing to ask for the amount they already had in mind, the gift was always closer to the target. Said Behn, "We began to see a pattern. Asking for a specific amount always proved to be the right choice."

"Solicitation training sessions and actual experiences encouraged our volunteers and got them thinking in new ways. Although it was difficult for some of them to get to a new place of asking, many did."

—SARA BEHN
EMPOWERMENT COORDINATOR
& DIRECTOR OF DEVELOPMENT

RESULTS:

The new Family Resource Center houses three programs: Adult Day Services, Day Care Center and Head Start. Adult Day Services provides daytime activities and meaningful social interaction for older adults who might otherwise spend most of the day alone. The accredited Day Care Center offers infant care and soon will provide child care beyond the regular workday, particularly important because 12 out of the 18 major employers in Boone operate more than one shift. The new facility also allows Head Start to expand its services from a half-day to full-day program.

Consultant's Tips

Consultant: Jean Kresse

Any solicitation, whether in writing—by letter, e-mail or web page—or face-to-face, requires an official "ask." The level of gift received—its size and the sentiment in which it is given—is greatly influenced by the method and motivation used to solicit that gift.

1. **Ask like you mean it.**

   A hesitant ask will likely prompt a hesitant gift. A confident ask will help produce a more impassioned gift.

2. **Be specific about the amount of the gift.**

   Once you ask for and receive a gift, you cannot add a quick addendum, "We appreciate this amount, but what we really had in mind was two more zeros at the end of this number." The door of opportunity has already swung shut behind you.

3. **Be specific about the nature of the gift.**

   A specific ask—how much the organization hopes to receive, how that amount can be given (cash and assets or a planned gift), and how it will be used (capital or endowment)—paves the way for realized expectations.

(continued on next page)

CONSULTANT'S TIPS (CONT.)

4. Ask for a realistic, but generous gift.

Always go in prepared to ask for a realistic, albeit generous gift. If the requested amount is too low, you not only leave money on the table, but you risk underestimating the financial worth and interest level of your prospective donor.

If you ask for an amount beyond what the donor has ever thought to give to the organization, you risk nothing. Either the donor will begin thinking differently about the organization, "They must really look to me as a valuable supporter" or give the largest amount he or she had in mind to give.

A solicitation is not the time for vagaries or half-hearted attempts. Donors appreciate forthrightness and clear expectations. Give donors a target. You will be pleased at how often they will meet and even exceed your expectations.

CHAPTER THREE

INTEGRATE CAMPAIGN ELEMENTS

"A billion here, a billion there, and pretty soon you are talking real money."

—Everett Dirksen

Lyric Opera of Kansas City

Kansas City, Missouri

CAMPAIGN NAME: "Realize the Vision"

CAMPAIGN TASK: To establish a permanent endowment and raise cash for immediate enhancements to programming in order to attain higher levels of artistic expression.

ORIGINAL CAMPAIGN GOAL: $10 million

AMOUNT RAISED: $11.5 million

LENGTH OF CAMPAIGN: 42 months

GENERAL DIRECTOR: Evan R. Luskin

DIRECTOR OF DEVELOPMENT: Michelle LaPointe

Campaign Highlight:

Identifying donors with a capacity to give large gifts is only Act I, Scene I. For any campaign, a great story line also requires fundraisers to distinguish between donors who are more likely to give to endowment over programming, cash versus a planned gift, capital rather than operations. In doing just this, the Lyric Opera of Kansas City managed to implement one of the most quintessential examples of an Integrated Fundraising Campaign[SM] and make beautiful music in the process.

Mission:

The Lyric Opera of Kansas City exists to enrich the lives of people of all ages and backgrounds throughout the region by offering a broad repertoire of professional operatic experiences.

History:

Today's Lyric Opera of Kansas City wows audiences in a building constructed in the 1920s. It first served as an auditorium until the 1940s when it was purchased and used by the American Red Cross for blood collection during World War II. After the war, the building was sold and reopened as a theater, changing owners several times over the next several decades. The Lyric Opera began in Kansas City in the 1950s and moved to its current location in the 1970s. The group originally leased the theater and finally bought it in 1991.

THE CAMPAIGN FOR LYRIC OPERA OF KANSAS CITY:

"An important lesson for me in this campaign was the philosophy of an Integrated Fundraising Campaign[SM]. We kept hearing from the consultant, 'This kind of campaign strengthens a relationship with your donor base.' I began to realize the campaign was not separate from day-to-day development. It was a supplement to everything we were already doing," said Michelle LaPointe, director of development.

Organizations can manage to pull off a successful campaign while their annual funds dry up. Following the campaign they have capital to build infrastructure, but no money for operations. When this happens the campaign can be alive and kicking, while the organization is, frankly, struggling for air.

Fortunately, this was not the case for *Realize the Vision*. The campaign took short- and long-term needs into consideration right from the start.

> *"We entered this campaign with a fresh perspective. The Lyric had never attempted a campaign of this size. We started with the Lyric family—people we already knew had a strong interest in giving—and worked from there."*
>
> —JOYCE HOLLAND
> CAMPAIGN CO-CHAIR

Offered Evan Luskin, general director, "Many years ago we considered the possibility of establishing an endowment. The subject had been in the discussion phase for a long time." A $2 million gift set up in a Charitable Remainder Trust given by long-time supporters of the Opera helped catapult an endowment campaign from discussion to action.

Campaign Co-Chair Joyce Holland acknowledged, "We entered this campaign with a fresh perspective. The Lyric had never attempted a campaign of this size. We started with the Lyric family—people we already knew had a strong interest in giving—and worked from there."

Once the campaign was under way, the committee decided to add program enhancements on top of the original $10 million in endowment. By really listening during the cultivation process of the campaign, members of the committee realized donors wanted long-term financial strength for the Opera, but they were also motivated by some short-term, quickly realized benefits.

Good research and prospect identification produced superior solicitations. "Sometimes a prospect would say, 'I can't give now (for this or that reason)' or 'I can't give as much as I would like.' But we were never turned down for lack of interest," said Holland.

A wonderful million-dollar matching gift—with half-a-million earmarked for long-term endowment and half directed to immediate programming—opened up many new and exciting gift opportunities toward the end of the campaign.

Some donors were interested in giving to the education piece of the endowment. The Lyric provides programs for music and arts education in schools and throughout the community. Other donors wanted their money to go directly into immediate performance enhancements. Even among opera enthusiasts there are varieties of giving preferences. Consequently, there should be a wide array of giving opportunities.

A fundraiser who will really listen during cultivation meetings will hear, within a few minutes, clues as to where donors are most inclined to give. Two people can listen to the same donor. One will pick up on the information. The other will miss it. Fundraisers who discipline themselves to listen carefully for a donor's preferences and inclinations will be considerably more successful when it comes time to solicit a gift.

Realize the Vision came in over goal with $10.5 million raised for endowment and an additional $1 million designated for direct program enhancements.

"A 'campaign mentality' has truly been integrated into the Opera across the board. We understand now that even when the campaign is over, the work doesn't end. *Realize the Vision* has caused us to grow, but it was not a one-time event. Our annual fund, our donor relationships, everything is strengthened by having gone through the campaign process," said LaPointe.

> *"Realize the Vision has caused us to grow, but it was not a one-time event. Our annual fund, our donor relationships, everything is strengthened by having gone through the campaign process."*
>
> —MICHELLE LAPOINTE
> DIRECTOR OF DEVELOPMENT

RESULTS:

In addition to a $10.5 million endowment for the Lyric Opera's financial future, *Realize the Vision* provided capital for the Opera to immediately attract internationally celebrated talent. Following the campaign the Lyric opened its season with world-renowned mezzo-soprano Joyce DiDonato. "It certainly is among one of the top fees we have ever paid. This is just an example of the quality of programs we'll be able to offer in the future," said Luskin.

CONSULTANT'S TIPS
CONSULTANT: ROBERT F. HARTSOOK, JD, EdD

An Integrated Fundraising Campaign℠ balances capital and endowment needs with annual development to ensure the greatest support for both. There's no sense in feeding a large capital campaign if annual operating funds are starved in the process. From campaign opening night to its closing finale, an Integrated Fundraising Campaign℠ takes this into consideration.

1. **"Don't rob Peter to pay Paul."**
   An Integrated Fundraising Campaign℠ will not put the squeeze on annual funds when the issue is addressed realistically and dealt with early on in the campaign.

2. **Listen carefully to what the donor is saying.**
   During the cultivation process prospective donors will often provide the information needed to help determine what gift(s) they would be willing to make.

3. **Identify prospective donors for each aspect of the campaign.**
   After listening carefully during cultivation visits, take the time to do additional prospect research. Know before going into a solicitation meeting what combination or types of giving a donor is open to consider.

Boy Scouts of America, Heart of America Council

Kansas City, Missouri

CAMPAIGN NAME: "Keeping Our Promise"

CAMPAIGN TASK: The continued growth of the Council's camping program has stressed the capacity of the Council's two summer camps. As well, facilities are aging and in need of repair or replacement. Of the capital raised, $6 million will be used for additions and improvements to the H. Roe Bartle Scout Reservation near Osceola, Missouri. Another $6.5 million will support additions and improvements to the Theodore Naish Scout Reservation in Bonner Springs, Kansas. The Council also plans to expand its Starr Scout Service Center in Kansas City, Missouri, requiring about $600,000. An endowment of nearly $4 million will be committed to ongoing maintenance of the two camps and the service center.

ORIGINAL CAMPAIGN GOAL: $15.25 million

AMOUNT RAISED: $14.2 million (campaign still in progress at time of printing)

LENGTH OF CAMPAIGN: 36 months (14 months completed at time of printing)

SCOUT EXECUTIVE: Jim Terry

CAMPAIGN HIGHLIGHT:

This campaign used a team concept to send the right people into the right solicitation meetings. Thorough preparation and practice preceded every major solicitation.

MISSION:

It is the mission of the Heart of America Council to prepare the young people of eastern Kansas and western Missouri to make ethical choices over their lifetimes by instilling in them the values of the Scout Oath and Scout Law.

HISTORY:

British Lord Robert Baden-Powell founded the original Boy Scout movement in 1907 in England. Soon thereafter, Chicago publisher William Dickson Boyce, who had become interested in the movement while on a business trip in London, helped establish the organization in the United States. The Boy Scouts of America was incorporated on February 8, 1910 and chartered by Congress in 1916. The Heart of America Council, which serves 19 counties surrounding Kansas City, is one of the largest, most active and most successful Councils in the country. It or its predecessors have been serving the greater Kansas City area since 1910.

The Campaign for Boy Scouts of America, Heart of America Council:

From the moment they stepped off the plane in Tulsa until they entered the J.E. and L.E. Mabee Foundation meeting, the solicitation team used the time they had to prepare—again—for this very important appointment.

Said Scout Executive Jim Terry, "We headed right into an airport conference room and ran through the questions we expected would be asked. Once we were in the meeting things clicked. We had prepared an answer for every question they asked us. Nothing took us by surprise."

The Scout Motto is "Be Prepared." In this case, preparation paid off.

The campaign leaders selected the right people for the solicitation team. Everyone had a part to play. Each knew his role and planned accordingly. Depth and scope of experience and expertise gave the team an edge.

"We had a prepared script, the right people going into the meeting and the right people traveling along for pre-game coaching. It was clearly a successful team effort."

—Matthew J. Beem, CFRE
Consultant

"One person had a history in approaching the Mabee Foundation, all of us had a personal appreciation and understanding of the Scouting program, a few of us had years of success in major-gift fundraising," consultant Matthew Beem said. "We had a prepared script, the right people going into the meeting and the right people traveling along for pre-game coaching. It was clearly a successful team effort."

Rather than looking at the campaign as one large, multimillion-dollar venture, the *Keeping Our Promise* team made each new challenge the main focus. "Without losing sight of the ultimate goal," Beem said, "we always directed our attention and preparation toward the next solicitation."

In receiving its $1 million Mabee challenge grant—among the largest gifts dispensed by the foundation—the Heart of America Council proved solid preparation and a "win-one-at-a-time" philosophy was smart strategy.

"Our dry runs prior to a solicitation, particularly in the case of the Mabee Foundation grant, were part business meeting, part rehearsal," Beem said. "You have to play to the strength of each team member and each solicitation participant."

Never take for granted the value of painstaking preparation and practice. Once a solicitation is under way, it's too late to review notes. And it certainly is not the time to create an uncomfortable silence, fumbling through papers to answer an unexpected question.

The enthusiasm and readiness that the *Keeping Our Promise* campaign team carried into solicitations directly translated into confidence, positively influenced donors and ultimately added many major gifts to this campaign.

RESULTS:

Still in progress, *Keeping Our Promise* will enlarge and produce upgrades to the Council's camps and Service Center. The H. Roe Bartle Scout Reservation hosts boys and adult leaders throughout the summer. Expansion of the reservation will add much-needed capacity. The Theodore Naish Scout Reservation hosts the majority of the Council's Cub Scout and Webelos campers and a large number of Boy Scout campers each summer. Improvements to the camps and Service Center in Kansas City will greatly advance the Council's ability to provide excellent Scout programming.

"Our dry runs prior to a solicitation, particularly in the case of the Mabee Foundation grant, were part business meeting, part rehearsal. You have to play to the strength of each team member and each solicitation participant."

—MATTHEW J. BEEM, CFRE
CONSULTANT

CONSULTANT'S TIPS

CONSULTANT: MATTHEW J. BEEM, CFRE

For the very best major gift solicitations, employ lessons from Scouting.

1. A Scout is always prepared.

Preparation is essential to success. One cannot prepare for an event after the fact. Think out and plan well ahead.

Just as a Scout must pack and prepare for a variety of camping climates, a campaign leadership team must anticipate the "climate" of a solicitation and prepare for every possible outcome.

2. Scout Spirit.

A Scout troop works because the leaders set a personal example, plan ahead and carry out responsibilities to the best of their ability. In the same way, a campaign team will accomplish great things through adequate training, proper delegation and enthusiastic cooperation.

Everyone benefits when shared experience and information is used in combination with a strong sense of morale and leadership.

(continued on next page)

CONSULTANT'S TIPS (CONT.)

3. A Scout is ... trustworthy ... cheerful ... brave.

So many of the qualities encouraged and exemplified by the Scouting program carry over into good fundraising principles. For example, three of the 12 points of the Scout Law:

Trustworthy. "A Scout tells the truth." A campaign leadership team should not only be ready with the answers, but give clear and dependable information to prospective donors and foundation representatives.

Cheerful. "A Scout looks for the bright side of things." Campaign leadership members should remain positive during the ups and downs of a campaign. Willingly and diligently undertaking assigned tasks not only makes for a more pleasant campaign environment but also increases the odds of campaign success.

Brave. "A Scout can face danger even if he is afraid." Few people relish the solicitation experience—at least not initially. However, with proper training, a clear understanding of major-gift fundraising and adequate preparation, a solicitation can be bravely and boldly undertaken and successfully achieved.

The Adoption Exchange
Aurora, Colorado

CAMPAIGN NAME: "Making Dreams Come True"

CAMPAIGN TASK: To purchase and retrofit an existing building for the organization's offices and to establish endowment funds.

ORIGINAL CAMPAIGN GOAL: $1.2 million

AMOUNT RAISED: $1.8 million

LENGTH OF CAMPAIGN: 18 months

EXECUTIVE DIRECTOR: Dixie van de Flier Davis, EdD

DIRECTOR OF CAPITAL CAMPAIGN AND PLANNED GIVING: Shelbi Perry

CAMPAIGN HIGHLIGHT:

No matter how quickly a campaign pulls out of the gate or takes its first turn around the track, virtually every organization will experience a slow season. What a nonprofit does during a campaign lull will either help get things moving again or potentially bring the campaign to a standstill. Using proven lessons of discipline and persistence, The Adoption Exchange pushed through an inevitable fundraising pause and completed its winning campaign well over goal.

MISSION:

To ensure that all children have safety and permanence in their own homes. To provide the connection between families who adopt and children who wait.

HISTORY:

The Adoption Exchange grew out of an informal meeting of adoption professionals who met regularly and exchanged information and resources to help secure permanent homes for children in foster care. The organization was officially established in March 1983.

THE CAMPAIGN FOR THE ADOPTION EXCHANGE:

"On our first day as an organization, the very moment I plugged in the telephone, it started ringing. And it hasn't stopped ringing since," said Dixie van de Flier Davis, executive director.

The Adoption Exchange grew naturally out of a great need to see children in foster care moved out of temporary holding patterns and into loving, stable, forever homes. The organization grew rapidly from a few adoption professionals meeting informally to a clearinghouse of resources and information serving dozens of adoption agencies.

"On our first day as an organization, the very moment I plugged in the telephone, it started ringing. And it hasn't stopped ringing since."

—DIXIE VAN DE FLIER DAVIS, EdD
EXECUTIVE DIRECTOR

It is this group's passionate commitment to the mission that keeps staff and volunteers pushing through every challenge and overcoming every obstacle. Said consultant Arliss Swartzendruber, "What stands out in my mind is this organization's commitment to children. They are so dedicated to their mission. It is that powerful message that helps motivate donors to give."

But even with a compelling mission and dedicated supporters, The Adoption Exchange experienced a slow season in its campaign that called for perseverance and determination to keep things on track.

Nonprofits are fraught with so many needs and activities that it can be easy to turn attention away from a campaign and onto other projects—especially when things hit a slow patch.

One day, two days, a week goes by. Everyone stays busy with important work, but the business of fundraising gets put on hold. For a capital campaign, this is a detour that can quickly turn into a dead end. Fortunately for The Adoption Exchange, the leadership team was never willing to give in to that very subtle temptation to pull back from the hard work of fundraising.

Even though Davis and Shelbi Perry, the director of capital campaign and planned giving, had been advised by colleagues to "go it alone" on a campaign, they acknowledged that without counsel this would have been a difficult time. "We really needed help, especially when we weren't seeing results," said Davis. Their consultant encouraged them to keep up the consistency of campaign tasks even when things waned.

"Timing is important for donor solicitations," Swartzendruber explained. "If you continue to make calls and work hard to get the organization's story out, there are so many ways to overcome slow periods."

The Adoption Exchange kept an ongoing list of donors who showed a particularly strong interest in the organization. Some donors are willing to issue a challenge gift to breathe life into a campaign during a slow time. A matching opportunity also gives fundraisers an open door to reconnect with prospects who, for whatever reason, have not yet given a major gift to the campaign.

Sometimes prospects have just given a large gift to another organization or have a personal or business-related issue that precludes them from giving. Six months later, circumstances may change dramatically. A challenge gift allows the organization to return to some of these prospects with "great news" and another opportunity to be part of the campaign.

Often plateaus will surface near the end of a campaign—months and months of calls and solicitations, a buzz of excitement and then everything starts slowing down. That last leg can be one of the most difficult lulls to overcome.

> "When we reached a plateau in the campaign, it would have been very easy to turn our attention to other pressing matters, but we needed to stay focused."
>
> —DIXIE VAN DE FLIER DAVIS, EDD
> EXECUTIVE DIRECTOR

Perseverance is again in order. The last push of a campaign is a great time to revisit some of the organization's strongest supporters. There will often be two or three donors who really want to be part of an effort to put the campaign over the top. Share with them the impact and success the campaign has already experienced. Offer your closest supporters a chance to cross the finish line together.

"As we came down to the wire on a challenge gift, a board member, who had already made a stretch gift, came back and wrote another check for as much as she gave the first time," said Davis. "This gift made it possible for us to meet a wonderful challenge gift. It was very moving to me that this little group, that started out of the trunk of my car, had friends so confident in the organization's mission.

"When we reached a plateau in the campaign, it would have been very easy to turn our attention to other pressing matters, but we needed to stay focused."

"Whenever there is a lull in a campaign," offered Swartzendruber, "the best advice is to push through and continue to do the campaign work you've been doing all along. By faithfully continuing with what has worked in the past, you will be surprised how many times a gift will arrive to re-energize the campaign."

If you never quit working, if you keep doing the right things over and over, you will find—along with the inevitable disappointments and plateaus—many wonderful surprises that can help get things moving again and headed swiftly toward the final destination.

RESULTS:

On the surface *Making Dreams Come True* provided a permanent home for The Adoption Exchange. But the money saved through owning versus leasing translates directly into more children's dreams of adoption becoming reality. With rent at $78,000 a year, ownership equals the cost of 31 adoptions annually. The campaign doubled the organization's budget, created wonderful new programs and added much needed technology.

CONSULTANT'S TIPS

CONSULTANT: ARLISS SWARTZENDRUBER

Persistence pays off. Plateaus are not impassable. They are just part of the landscape on the way to the destination. If a campaign begins to show signs of slowing, take a tip from *Making Dreams Come True:*

1. **Continue doing what has worked in the past.**

2. **Maintain a list of donors** who might be willing to launch a challenge gift, and another of the prospects who might be interested in the good news of a challenge.

3. **Keep an ongoing list of strong supporters** who would enjoy being part of a last push to take the campaign over the top.

Girl Scouts– Bluestem Council

Bartlesville, Oklahoma

CAMPAIGN NAME: "Partners for the Future"

CAMPAIGN TASK: To expand and renovate the Kiwanis Park Program Center; to make significant facility improvements to the satellite office in Ponca City; and to make additions to the Council's 524-acre Camp Wah-Shah-She in Osage County.

ORIGINAL CAMPAIGN GOAL: $600,000

AMOUNT RAISED: $1.3 million

LENGTH OF CAMPAIGN: 24 months

EXECUTIVE DIRECTOR: Kimberly Lynch

DIRECTOR OF DEVELOPMENT: Tiffany Cowan

On my honor I will try: To serve God and my country, To help people at all times, And to live by the Girl Scout Law.

CAMPAIGN HIGHLIGHT:

This organization was willing to overcome some of the faulty game plans and false assumptions nonprofits have about fundraising. "We can earn what we need if we sell enough stuff." "We can get a thousand people to each give a hundred dollars." "We can put a thermometer sign downtown to show how much money we need," and so on. Instead, this Council decided to try something new and in the process began to dream big dreams for the organization. Even though they serve some of the poorest counties in their region, members of the Council took a bold step away from old ways of thinking about fundraising and leaned into a new future for the organization and the many girls they serve.

MISSION:

To inspire girls with the highest ideals of character, conduct, patriotism and service so that they may become happy and resourceful citizens.

HISTORY:

The Girl Scouts was started by Juliette Low in 1912. By 1920, Girl Scouts was growing and had added its own uniform, handbook, constitution and bylaws. Cookie sales began in 1936. The first known Girl Scout troop in the area dates back to between 1914 and 1918. Bluestem Council received its charter in 1941.

THE CAMPAIGN FOR GIRL SCOUTS—BLUESTEM COUNCIL:

Some organizations have a long history of generating money through events, sales, contracts or annual contributions from a large agency. The regularity and repetitive nature of this money can wear a rut in the road when it comes to major gift fundraising. "This is how we've always made our money. Why should we take on the added effort of a campaign?"

The Girls Scouts–Bluestem Council understood that cookie sales were a permanent feature of the Girl Scouts program. The cookie project not only generated profits, but it was a good way for girls to practice the skills of communication, organization and responsibility. Besides, try telling neighbors they will have to forego their Caramel Delites or Classic Shortbread—there could be rioting in the streets.

The Bluestem Council recognized the limitations of cookie sales to produce the big money necessary for making capital repairs, additions or long strides in programming. They wanted to deliver the positive effects of Girl Scouting to a greater number of girls, especially those with little access to the program. That would require a lot of cookies—or one very successful capital campaign.

> *"Raising funds for a great organization can actually be fun. It is one of the most satisfying things you can do. I began the process with less positive feelings about fundraising, but my confidence increased through the process."*
>
> —PAT ROMINES
> CAMPAIGN CO-CHAIR

"The challenge many organizations have is that they get stuck thinking about one or two streams of income. Hospitals and mental health groups have contracts with state and local agencies. School groups sell calendars and discount cards door to door. When they need money, they tend to run back to what they know," said consultant Robert Swanson.

Bluestem Council was ahead of the curve in understanding the difference between sales and securing major gifts. Organizations that have not had to depend on philanthropy in the past find it hard to make the transition. In contrast, this group readily accepted a new approach to fundraising and learned quickly.

"Raising funds for a great organization can actually be fun. It is one of the most satisfying things you can do. I began the process with less positive feelings about fundraising, but my confidence increased through the process," said Campaign Co-Chair Pat Romines.

They also managed to see the campaign in a new light. Said Romines, "Initially, we were only going to raise enough to get by. Our consultant advised us to determine what was actually needed before we went to the community with our story."

Another textbook obstacle for campaign volunteers is hesitancy or resistance in asking for major gifts. Volunteers should be reminded that a solicitation isn't about them. It is a very objective process. Volunteers take the message of the organization and faithfully, accurately and repeatedly deliver it to prospects and donors. Whether or not donors give is entirely up to them. It is not about the person who asks for the gift. It is about lives changed for the better. It is about being *Partners for the Future.*

In the end, the Bluestem Council campaign enjoyed a respectable blend of individual, corporate, foundation and trust gifts. They were very successful at stretch gifts. The leadership team and volunteers helped people see the benefits of philanthropy. In fact, several donors made their single largest gift ever to this campaign.

Through a willingness to "think outside the cookie box" and learn the fundraising process necessary to solicit major gifts, the Council stepped into a new place of financial stability and community visibility

Said Romines, "One of the greatest benefits of a campaign is that it gives an organization a chance to tell its story to the community. We had a powerful volunteer base, but a volunteer and a donor base are quite different. *Partners for the Future* allowed us to develop and expand our donor base, which strengthened the organization and, consequently, helps us reach and serve a greater number of girls."

> *"One of the greatest benefits of a campaign is that it gives an organization a chance to tell its story to the community."*
>
> —Pat Romines
> Campaign Co-Chair

Results:

Improvements to the Ponca City facility, additions to Camp Wah-Shah-She, and a larger, renovated Kiwanis Park Program Center give the organization a greater ability to reach out to underserved populations of girls in the area—minority girls, girls with disabilities, girls from low-income families and girls who have minimal parental support. *Partners for the Future* helped make that possible.

CONSULTANT'S TIPS

CONSULTANT: ROBERT G. SWANSON

Major gift fundraising is not about selling things. It is about creating a donor base that understands and supports the organization's mission.

1. Cookies are not fundraising.

Cookie sales are a signature event for the Girl Scouts. As such, they will always be a vital part of the organization. However, for capital improvements, endowments and growing programs, cookie sales (bake sales, quilt auctions, popcorn sales, etc.) will never meet all the needs.

2. Nobody wants to give money away.

Donors are not looking for a way to unload their money. However, if donors are interested in what an organization is accomplishing in the lives of people, they can become excited about investing their money in that work. This is the work of fundraising, connecting a particular mission with an interested, qualified donor.

3. Set a campaign goal that meets the organization's long-term objectives.

A nonprofit willing to undertake a capital campaign should set its sights at funding realistic, but significantly long-term, goals. Donors want to be part of something great. If the bar is set too low, a group may find themselves in the unenviable position of revisiting donors for help with needs that should have been addressed in the original goal.

CHAPTER FOUR

SUCCESS BRINGS SUCCESS

"Recognize the true needs of your prospects—and respond to them creatively."

—Eric Baron

Inter-Faith Ministries

Wichita, Kansas

CAMPAIGN NAME: "Heart to Heart"

CAMPAIGN TASK: To purchase and renovate buildings for a program and ministry center, to add a homeless shelter, erase debt and create an endowment.

ORIGINAL CAMPAIGN GOAL: $1 million

AMOUNT RAISED: $3 million

LENGTH OF CAMPAIGN: 24 months

EXECUTIVE DIRECTOR: Sam Muyskens

CAMPAIGN HIGHLIGHT:

Before a nonprofit can attract major gifts, it is important to first assess the general perceptions and impressions people have about the organization. Inter-Faith Ministries (IFM) took this critical step and developed a strategy to build on its positive reputation while addressing issues of concern. An integrated campaign helped IFM transform its precampaign reputation as a group always in dire straits into a financially rock-solid nonprofit.

MISSION:

To build inter-religious understanding, promote justice, relieve misery and reconcile the estranged ... offer hope, healing and understanding.

HISTORY:

Inter-Faith Ministries began as an alliance of Protestant Christian leaders in 1885. In 1919, the Ministerial Alliance was renamed the Wichita Council of Churches. Roman Catholic, Orthodox and Jewish congregations joined the Council in the 1930s. To reflect its inclusiveness among diverse religious groups, the organization changed its name to Inter-Faith Ministries in 1978.

THE CAMPAIGN FOR INTER-FAITH MINISTRIES:

"Inter-Faith Ministries' executive director made a decision to learn how to become a major gift fundraiser. His willingness to accept mentoring meant a new day for the organization financially," said consultant Bob Hartsook.

For years IFM had accepted the idea that "nonprofit" meant "no money." It is a typical misconception among not-for-profit groups, particularly those such as Inter-Faith Ministries that serve low-income and indigent populations.

IFM had provided food, shelter, medical care and education for decades. It also served as a safety net for the homeless in the area, offering services to accommodate individuals who did not meet the criteria of other agencies.

"We knew we had to look at something different. Our board met and decided we would try something big."

—SAM MUYSKENS
EXECUTIVE DIRECTOR

Although IFM was well-known for its sacrificial and tireless work, pro-active and positively positioned fundraising had never been a standard practice among staff and supporters. Over the years a mounting debt reached $100,000. Said Executive Director Sam Muyskens, "'Crisis fundraising' was no longer feasible.

"We knew we had to look at something different. Our board met and decided we would try something big." A campaign would certainly qualify as something big.

INTER-FAITH MINISTRIES

Said Muyskens, "Bob recommended that we not begin actively seeking funds until we completed a preliminary campaign assessment to help us determine exactly where we were headed. We interviewed political and religious leaders to find out how we were viewed in the community. We found that people thought of us as a program of dignity, but one that was always in financial difficulty."

Desperation fundraising had become more than a way of life; it had become part of the organization's identity. This needed to change—and fast.

Even though a homeless shelter was an immediate and important need, IFM took expert advice and chose to first get its own financial house in order. IFM opted to put other projects on hold and focus on a fund primarily underwritten by board members to eliminate the debt.

Once the debt was behind them, IFM leaders set out to identify potential major donors and new giving opportunities. In addition to approaching individuals, corporations and foundations for gifts, IFM looked into a state program available to qualifying groups.

"We applied for and received State of Kansas tax credits and were awarded a $350,000 contribution toward the campaign and received some very large gifts from area businesses and individuals," said Muyskens. "Needless to say, a couple of major gifts help give credibility to an organization. We found that visiting with the local businesses and organizations was paying off. We also discovered that when we asked, people responded."

Moving from debt to distinction meant discipline, hard work and a willingness to do the right things in the right order.

Trying something new, "something big," as Muyskens described it, is something not every organization is willing to attempt. Inter-Faith Ministries not only managed to shift its operations and reputation from "crisis mode" to "well managed," it increased its ability to serve others as well.

Admitted Muyskens, "Although I never considered myself a fundraiser, I now have a better understanding about the process. I discovered that fundraising is not such a daunting task. I am no longer inhibited by the intricacies. I am proud of what we have accomplished at Inter-Faith Ministries and believe wholeheartedly in our mission."

> *"Although I never considered myself a fundraiser, I now have a better understanding about the process...*
> *I am proud of what we have accomplished at Inter-Faith Ministries and believe wholeheartedly in our mission."*
>
> —Sam Muyskens
> Executive Director

Results:

Not only was its long-standing debt erased, but in addition to an endowment securing the organization's financial future, Inter-Faith Ministries was able to acquire three buildings to be used by its various programs. Moreover, *Heart to Heart* changed the way the organization thinks about itself and views its impact on the community. Last but not least, experiencing a successful campaign forever changed the way IFM thinks about philanthropy and major gift fundraising.

CONSULTANT'S TIPS
CONSULTANTS: ROBERT F. HARTSOOK, JD, EdD
& ROBERT G. SWANSON

Before undertaking a campaign, an organization must positively position itself to receive significant funding.

1. **Take down the "going out of business" sign.**
   Reject a "crisis fundraising" mentality. Donors may be willing to bail a nonprofit out once, but it cannot become the fundraising modus operandi.

2. **Test the waters.**
   Thoroughly assess the organization's reputation among donors, community leaders, area residents and other organizations.

3. **Learn a new skill (or two, or three ...)**
   Be willing to embrace new ways of thinking about raising money. Become a good student of the art of identifying, cultivating and asking donors for major gifts.

The Salvation Army of Topeka

Topeka, Kansas

CAMPAIGN NAME: "Need Knows No Season"

CAMPAIGN TASK: Renovate and expand the Topeka Corps facility to meet increased social service and child-care needs.

ORIGINAL CAMPAIGN GOAL: $3.75 million

AMOUNT RAISED: $3.9 million

LENGTH OF CAMPAIGN: 27 months

DIVISIONAL DIRECTOR OF DEVELOPMENT: Roger Alexander

COMMANDER: Captain Paul Duskin

CAMPAIGN HIGHLIGHT:

The Salvation Army is known for taking on the most difficult challenges in a community. The Army regularly moves into the poorest parts of town and establishes themselves where other organizations and businesses have shied away. This willingness to serve in the hardest hit areas was not lost on its Topeka neighbors. *Need Knows No Season* managed to involve the entire city by initiating a number of creative strategies. The Salvation Army of Topeka had not attempted a capital campaign since 1965. But when it came time to take on this new enterprise, it met the challenge in true Salvation Army fashion—committed, positive and openhearted. Its ability to use creative methods for taking the campaign public drew broad community support and took them above and beyond the campaign goal.

MISSION:

To preach the gospel of Jesus Christ and to meet human needs in His name without discrimination.

HISTORY:

In 1865 a Methodist minister, William Booth, founded The Salvation Army in England. By 1880 the organization had reached across the Atlantic to eastern cities in the United States. The Salvation Army of Topeka began in 1886.

THE CAMPAIGN FOR THE SALVATION ARMY OF TOPEKA:

"Every day The Salvation Army of Topeka battles poverty, violence, substance abuse and despair. Over time the facility had become extremely outdated and woefully inadequate. This greatly curtailed its ability to deliver a wide array of human services in a dignified and efficient way. Faced with rapidly growing demands for services, the board agreed to launch a capital campaign to purchase and renovate a new facility," said Kris Robbins, campaign chair.

Added consultant Susan Schneweis, "In 30 years, the agency had not asked the Topeka community for capital funding. Decades of service had been provided—food, rent and utility assistance, clothing, counseling, prescriptions, personal care items, eye exams and so on. As the campaign proved, the Topeka community was grateful and extremely supportive of everything they did." *Need Knows No Season* gave Topeka a forum to demonstrate gratitude.

"We wanted to see The Salvation Army operating out of a new facility that allowed it to expand programming and maintain its heritage of selfless service—and we wanted to see this work continue for another 100 years."

—KRIS ROBBINS
CAMPAIGN CHAIR

Offered Robbins, "We wanted to see The Salvation Army operating out of a new facility that allowed it to expand programming and maintain its heritage of selfless service—and we wanted to see this work continue for another 100 years."

Corporate, foundation and individual gifts took the campaign within reach of its goal. With 80 percent raised and well within range of the target goal—only $750,000 outstanding—the organization decided to make an official announcement.

When The Salvation Army was ready to go public with the campaign, it was announced in the *Topeka Capital-Journal*. The timing was right to have the full-page article run to coincide with Mother's Day. The Salvation Army does so much for children and families the association seemed especially appropriate.

By including an envelope and an ask inside each paper, every Topeka resident was invited to help finish off the campaign. The envelope strategy, in conjunction with a direct appeal to former Salvation Army donors, brought in $50,000 in four weeks.

Kettle donations—a Salvation Army signature event—were low. The campaign was coming to a close, but The Salvation Army had not yet reached goal. How could it boost kettle donations and at the same time help bring the campaign to a successful conclusion? A campaign chair, whose company had already given a major gift, offered another creative idea for spicing things up. He challenged the whole community to join in. If $5,000 came in to the kettles on a given day, his company would match that amount dollar for dollar.

Ongoing radio announcements let the community know about this exciting challenge and told them where the kettles were located around town. Offered Schneweis, "You better believe volunteers were counting the money in those kettles throughout the day."

In just one day, donations, plus the matching gift, produced $10,000 for *Need Knows No Season*. Not only did both of these communitywide creative strategies generate money, they drew new friends to the organization, increased visibility and gave the whole city an opportunity to show its gratitude for The Salvation Army.

Capital campaigns require a lot of hard work and dedication. Adding some creativity, especially if it involves a wider circle of donors and raises community awareness in the process, can give a traditional campaign a helping hand.

"You better believe volunteers were counting the money in those kettles throughout the day."

—SUSAN SCHNEWEIS
CONSULTANT

RESULTS:

The campaign tripled the size of The Salvation Army of Topeka's facility from 11,000 square feet to more than 34,000 square feet. The child-care building expanded to care for more than 130 children, when before it provided space for only 82. Improved security features and a new playground were also added to the facility. A 5,000-square-foot warehouse was added to increase and improve food distribution. Changes to the building enhanced services and helped revitalize a low-income section of Topeka.

CONSULTANT'S TIPS

CONSULTANT: SUSAN SCHNEWEIS

People are more motivated to give when appropriately and adequately challenged. The Salvation Army of Topeka demonstrated creativity and smart strategies to finish its goal.

1. **Do not go public prematurely.**
   By waiting until it had secured 80 percent of the goal, the organization was able to ensure its public perception of success. Winners attract the attention and support of others. Once the community was invited to be part of a winning team, the residents were prepped and ready.

2. **Be willing to try something new.**
   Take a traditional campaign and add a personal touch. Take a challenge, such as the last push of a campaign, and add a creative strategy—a communitywide challenge or matching gift.

3. **Celebrate success.**
   Share the victory of a successful campaign using a public forum—newspapers, radio, TV spots. Positive visibility can help uncover new volunteers and prospective donors for the future.

Lensic Performing Arts Center

Santa Fe, New Mexico

CAMPAIGN NAME: "The Lensic Performing Arts Center Capital Campaign"

CAMPAIGN TASK: To convert a 70-year-old movie theater into an elegant, multifaceted performing arts center to meet myriad performance needs in this arts community.

ORIGINAL CAMPAIGN GOAL: $8 million

AMOUNT RAISED: $9.2 million

LENGTH OF CAMPAIGN: 36 months

GENERAL MANAGER: Robert Martin

CAMPAIGN HIGHLIGHT:

When opportunity knocks, enlist a great committee to open the door. The Lensic's steering committee went well beyond the simple assignment of cultivating and soliciting donors. The committee tailored its message to specific donor demographics, fine-tuned cultivation and elevated solicitation to an art form.

MISSION:

The Lensic, Santa Fe's performing arts center, provides citizens of New Mexico with diverse, year-round programming. It also serves as a center for community use and civic events, and is committed to providing sponsorships and educational programs. The Lensic supports local and national artists and offers a unique cross-cultural experience for audiences of all ages.

HISTORY:

The Lensic Theater first opened in 1931 as a film and vaudeville house. Built by Nathan Salmon, along with his son-in-law E. John Greer, the Lensic was the finest theater of its time in the Southwest. After a long list of owners and decades of use as a movie theater, the Lensic was transformed into its current role as the Lensic Performing Arts Center—not only meeting a community need for performance space, but adding to the rejuvenation of downtown Santa Fe.

THE CAMPAIGN FOR THE LENSIC PERFORMING ARTS CENTER:

When you undertake a campaign of this magnitude, it is important to start with a superior committee. The Lensic's leadership team was creative and enthusiastic. They employed innovative means for cultivating donor relationships and uncovering major gifts.

Nancy Zeckendorf, the Lensic's steering committee chair, knew from the beginning what an undertaking this project would be. She had just completed a successful campaign for the Santa Fe Opera, so she was familiar with the practicalities of a major campaign venture. "Of course, if I'd known that the final goal would be over $9 million, I might never have started," Zeckendorf mused. "Yet, as I look back, I'm glad I was involved in this wonderful work."

> *"Of course, if I'd known that the final goal would be over $9 million, I might never have started. Yet, as I look back, I'm glad I was involved in this wonderful work."*
>
> —NANCY ZECKENDORF
> CAMPAIGN CHAIR

The thought of turning the Lensic into a modern performing arts center had been a longtime dream of many Santa Fe residents. "People had been talking about this for decades," Zeckendorf said. "My greatest concern was that someone would begin the process without recognizing how important it was for the theater adaptations to include all the performing arts."

What was extraordinary about this steering committee was the way it identified particular pockets of donors—subspecialties—and tailored cultivation to reach these groups of people. Added counsel Susan Thomas, "In some instances, it was like having a campaign within a campaign."

For example, volunteers helped oversee cultivation events for "Texas prospects." Receptions, cocktail parties and dinners for Texans, by Texans (with homes in Santa Fe), allowed the Lensic to present its case in ways these prospects were most comfortable and compelled to hear.

Cultivation within the Santa Fe business community took a different tactic: Businesses would benefit from the activity generated by the Lensic. Business leaders were also very interested in the campaign, but they needed different kinds of information. Local government also needed to be addressed in a special way. Said Zeckendorf, "In order to increase the height of the theater and push back one wall, we needed a nod from the City. We really required their full cooperation."

Similarly, the neighbor constituency had its own unique interests and desires concerning the Lensic's transformation. Performing arts groups had a variety of other questions about the campaign, and so on.

Great consensus about the many benefits that the Lensic brought to the community grew as the campaign progressed. Santa Fe arts groups, business executives and the many individuals devoted to the arts and institutions all found common ground.

One building—many donor interests. And all along the way the campaign committee recognized there were a multitude of methods needed to cultivate and solicit gifts—different ways to approach donors, different interests, different sensitivities, and one very successful campaign.

RESULTS:

The opening of the Lensic as a performing arts center has filled a number of needs in the community. Prior to the Lensic capital campaign, Santa Fe was an "arts center" without a performing arts venue. There was no single place for all the performing arts—dance, opera, theater, orchestral, film and so on—to provide the pleasure of their productions to a grateful Santa Fe audience. Before the Lensic's transformation, production groups were forced to rent less-than-adequate auditoriums and deal with unending logistical challenges. Thankfully, this is no longer the case.

"My greatest concern was that someone would begin the process without recognizing how important it was for the theater adaptations to include all the performing arts."

—NANCY ZECKENDORF
CAMPAIGN CHAIR

In addition to enhanced performances, the renovated Lensic Performing Arts Center has brought added vitality to downtown Santa Fe. Both as a cultural and business boon for the city of Santa Fe, the Lensic's capital improvements have helped create fresh interest in the downtown area.

CONSULTANT'S TIPS

CONSULTANT: SUSAN DUNCAN THOMAS, CFRE

Some campaigns have the power to capture the imagination of a whole city. An ability to connect specific demographics with the right cultivation and information will greatly advance campaign efforts.

1. **Look for subspecialties.**
   Identify subsets of donors—people who have more in common than just the organization.

2. **Gather the right information.**
   Anticipate the particular questions and interests of these various groups.

3. **Create a buzz.**
   Use small group events to bring these like-minded people together to rally around the same cause.

Of course, each donor is unique and should be treated as such, but there are also pockets of donors who can be effectively reached by considering their shared interests in the campaign.

Children's Center Campus

Kansas City, Missouri

CAMPAIGN NAME: "Children's Center Campus Campaign"

CAMPAIGN TASK: To design and construct a 50,000-square-foot facility to be shared by three children's organizations: Children's Center for the Visually Impaired (CCVI), Children's TLC (TLC), and day-care provider (YWCA)*.

* The current day-care provider, the YMCA, stepped into this function in 2002.

ORIGINAL CAMPAIGN GOAL: $11 million

AMOUNT RAISED: $11.6 million

LENGTH OF CAMPAIGN: 30 months

EXECUTIVE DIRECTORS:
CCVI—Mary Lynne Dolembo
TLC—Shirley Patterson, PhD

CAMPAIGN HIGHLIGHT:

The Children's Center Campus is an example of positive collaboration between like-minded organizations. Three non-profits—one facility. Through open discussion, foresight and cooperation, these children's groups successfully navigated a smart course of action and arrived at a mutually advantageous destination.

MISSION:

Children's Center for the Visually Impaired—To prepare children with visual impairments, including those with multiple disabilities, to function at their highest potential in the sighted world.

Children's TLC (Therapeutic Learning Center)—To provide therapeutic and educational intervention through a team approach for children with disabilities from birth through eight years of age. Family-centered services are utilized to increase each child's functional abilities and prepare the child for a successful transition into the school environment.

HISTORY:

CCVI—The organization began in 1952 as the Kansas City Nursery School for the Blind. After several name changes, it took the designation Children's Center for the Visually Impaired in 1982.

TLC—Children's TLC started in 1947 as the Cerebral Palsy Nursery School. The organization changed its name in 1956 to Crippled Children's Nursery School. It was renamed Children's TLC (Therapeutic Learning Center) in 1991 with expanded services including early learning intervention for infants and toddlers.

THE CAMPAIGN FOR CHILDREN'S CENTER CAMPUS:

Something very important had to occur before the three organizations entered into a collaborative agreement. They first had to realistically assess the needs of their respective organizations and acknowledge the nature of nonprofit fundraising.

The similarity of TLC and CCVI's missions created an environment for competition (vying for some of the same philanthropic dollars) or the potential for mutual support. With new nonprofits popping up every year, organizations are beginning to recognize the value of avoiding duplicated services. Not only does this make good business sense, foundations and donors appreciate the conservation and stewardship of available resources.

> *"We wanted to have a day care in place which would provide peer models of typically developing kids. We felt the interaction among all the kids would be very beneficial."*
>
> —MARY LYNNE DOLEMBO
> EXECUTIVE DIRECTOR, CCVI

There is no question that the nonprofit sector is on the rise. The number of U.S. nonprofits nearly doubled during the last quarter of the 20th century. *The New Nonprofit Almanac IN BRIEF* estimates 74 percent growth just in 501(c)3 organizations from 1987 to 1998. The number of all nonprofits grew from 1.3 million to 1.6 million during the same decade.

According to *The Chronicle of Philanthropy*, "In many parts of the country today, there are simply too many non-profits. The plain fact is that having an excessive number of nonprofit organizations actually weakens the collective power of the entire field."

Rather than go it alone, TLC and CCVI joined forces to create a wonderful environment where children—even those with significant limitations—could laugh, learn and feel loved. In considering a shared facility—to be called the Children's Campus Center (CCC)—the leadership of both groups recognized another obvious need.

Virtually all of the children they served had siblings without disabilities. For families with children at TLC and CCVI who also had children in day care elsewhere, this meant parents had to drop off and pick up at several different locations around town. "We wanted to have a day care in place which would provide peer models of typically developing kids," says Mary Lynne Dolembo, executive director of CCVI. "We felt the interaction among all the kids would be very beneficial."

By inviting another organization to the table to provide day care to the general population, the three groups could now share space, avoid duplication of services, cooperate in the course of major gift fundraising and make life a whole lot easier for some very grateful families in the process.

Finding common ground between the three organizations required significant foresight and planning. Said Dolembo, "Our consultant helped us establish a strategic alliance agreement. We developed guidelines, prepared lease agreements and essentially covered all the bases legally." Three board members from each organization came together to form a separate Children's Center Campus Board of Directors.

"Several major donors insisted that they would not be supportive if creating CCC meant feeding another nonprofit," said consultant Bob Hartsook. The three directors worked cooperatively in fundraising. They were very clear and up-front with funders about the structure and organization of the Center.

Once prospective donors were identified as having a capacity to give and an interest in one or all of the groups, the representative with the best donor connection was sent to make a major gift solicitation.

> *"The fact that we were continually presenting ourselves as a team was positive. People saw that we were united."*
>
> —SHIRLEY PATTERSON, PhD
> EXECUTIVE DIRECTOR, TLC

TLC Executive Director Shirley Patterson admitted, "There were some differences of opinion. They were primarily operational and philosophical, obviously not of the magnitude to stop the project. The fact that we were continually presenting ourselves as a team was positive. People saw that we were united."

Rather than contend over some of the same funding, these children's groups modeled what they surely teach the children they serve. "It's nice to share."

RESULTS:

The new Children's Campus Center offers a therapeutic pool, cafeteria and kitchen, reception and waiting areas, meeting and conference rooms, and gymnasiums. This unique partnership gives the agencies an opportunity to share resources without losing their distinct identities. By placing three autonomous children's organizations in close proximity, the Children's Campus Center has the added benefit of promoting interaction and understanding between children of varying abilities and limitations.

CONSULTANT'S TIPS

CONSULTANT: ROBERT F. HARTSOOK, JD, EdD

Open discussion and ongoing cooperation can yield a win-win outcome (or in this case, a win-win-win outcome) for compatible nonprofits. The three groups followed some very basic lessons in order to achieve this exceptional level of unity—lessons they share with the children they serve.

1. Tell the truth.
Be open and honest not only with each other, but also with donors and volunteers. Be up front about what will change and what will remain the same. Be clear on how donor gifts will be shared or distributed.

2. Play fair.
Try to negotiate an agreement that is mutually beneficial. Look out for the interests of your organization, but not at the detriment of a collaborating nonprofit. If you see a potential inequity, for your organization or another group involved, point it out.

3. Have fun.
The synergy of groups or individuals working together toward one objective can be extraordinary. Collaboration can be an exhilarating process if everyone stays focused on the mutual goal.

Kansas Trial Lawyers Association

Topeka, Kansas

CAMPAIGN NAME: "Legacy of Justice"

CAMPAIGN TASK: To renovate a historic Topeka building to serve as the association headquarters, establish an education and resource center within the facility, and build an endowment. The site selected, standing in the shadow of the state Capitol, was a 13,000-square-foot, two-story fire station built in 1927.

ORIGINAL CAMPAIGN GOAL: $1 million set by the board

AMOUNT RAISED: $2.4 million

LENGTH OF CAMPAIGN: 30 months

EXECUTIVE DIRECTOR: Terry Humphrey

DIRECTOR OF DEVELOPMENT: Chris Keeshan

CAMPAIGN HIGHLIGHT:

Cultivation and solicitation should always be personalized to the prospect. The Kansas Trail Lawyers Association took that lesson to heart. KTLA's creativity and tenacity in securing major gifts was extraordinary.

MISSION:

To improve the legal profession through education, support and guidance by raising the standards of advocacy and trial practice; and secure justice for all by promoting safety, demanding accountability and preserving the right to trial by jury.

HISTORY:

The Kansas Trial Lawyers Association was established in 1952 from an earlier group called the Kansas Association of Plaintive Attorneys. KTLA was headquartered in Topeka's Colombian Building before moving to the Jayhawk Towers and finally to a permanent home in its new facility.

The Campaign for Kansas Trial Lawyers Association:

The Kansas Trial Lawyers Association is committed to preserving and strengthening the laws that make Kansas safer for families. So it seemed entirely appropriate that KTLA would choose to restore a historic fire station as its headquarters.

A less obvious connection is trial lawyers and philanthropy. As one said during the campaign, "If a group of lawyers can raise this much money, they must believe it to be a very important cause."

"As a 501(c) 6 organization—an association—philanthropy was not a familiar activity for the members of this organization," consultant Robert Swanson said. "The staff and campaign leadership committee deserve credit for stepping out of their comfort zone."

Said Director of Development Chris Keeshan, "We were aggressive about asking potential donors for gifts. We put a lot of time and effort into getting to know our prospects before we ever met with them. By the time we sat down with someone, we already knew quite a bit about that person—hobbies, lifestyle, hometown, family, values, giving history—

> *"We put a lot of time and effort into getting to know our prospects before we ever met with them. By the time we sat down with someone, we already knew quite a bit about that person—hobbies, lifestyle, hometown, family, values, giving history—everything we possibly could."*
>
> —Chris Keeshan
> Director of Development

everything we possibly could. Without this insight, we would not have been as successful in our ability to present a persuasive case for support. Good preparation also allowed us to be creative."

The best example of KTLA's creativity was in cultivating and soliciting a prospect that lived out of the state. This man was known for his great sense of humor. He had been cultivated face to face in the past, but when it came time to ask for a gift, it was difficult to arrange a meeting. He traveled extensively, but was not anticipating a return to Kansas for a very long time. Everyone understood that a major gift solicitation should not be made in a letter. And yet, the ask had to be made.

Using the extensive information they had gathered about this particular individual, they adapted their presentation to fit his personality. "We sent a video of KTLA members he knew giving amusing appeals," offered Keeshan. Since they knew he was a big tennis buff, they placed his picture inside a tennis racket so he was also featured in the video. While this could have been the worst idea for the majority of other prospects, good research and an ability to read an individual made this solicitation a huge success.

The video demonstrated that KTLA not only knew something about him, it conveyed a congenial and reciprocal message, "We know you. We like you. And we hope you like us, too." Clearly he did. His gift of $100,000 was followed by a second major gift later on in the campaign.

Cultivation and personalized solicitation were not only important ingredients in the *Legacy of Justice* campaign; they proved essential. Said Keeshan, "Two lessons I learned through this campaign were the importance of teaching people to be risk takers in asking for gifts and to go in with all the right information. Knowing as much as you can about the prospect allows you to not only be confident in asking for a gift, but it gives you the opportunity to be prepared for each unique situation.

RESULTS:

The restored Fire Station No. 2—used as a fire station and headquarters for the Topeka Fire Department until 1979—is now designated as a Topeka landmark to be placed on the National Historic Register. In its new role as the KTLA headquarters, the facility provides members and the public a place to research, obtain information and gain a greater understanding of the civil justice system. With the new headquarters, the organization is better able to train and educate plaintiffs' attorneys, law students and consumers. The facility includes administrative space for KTLA staff, conference rooms, deposition and meeting rooms, and the Robert K. Weary Education Center.

> *"Knowing as much as you can about the prospect allows you to not only be confident in asking for a gift, but it gives you the opportunity to be prepared for each unique situation."*
>
> —CHRIS KEESHAN
> DIRECTOR OF DEVELOPMENT

CONSULTANT'S TIPS

CONSULTANT: ROBERT G. SWANSON

A solicitation without an ask is just a visit. Visiting is part of cultivation and an important part of the process, but solicitation is a defining moment. When soliciting a gift:

1. **Make it memorable.**
   Be creative and demonstrative about the ask.

2. **Make it personal.**
   Tailor each solicitation to match the prospect's personality and interests.

3. **Make it clear and concise.**
   Get to the point and make the point crystal clear. "We would like you to consider making a gift of (fill in the blank) dollars to (fill in the blank)."

Fundraising should include having "fun." Sure, there is a lot of hard work along the way, but do not get so bogged down in the details that you miss opportunities to be creative and enjoy the process.

Chapter Five

Building Your Base of Support

"Every move must have a purpose."

—*Bruce Pandolfini*

Exploration Place

Wichita, Kansas

CAMPAIGN NAME: "Extraordinary Futures Start Here"

CAMPAIGN TASK: To build a science and exploration center; to fund new exhibits, programs, and staffing; and to create an endowment.

ORIGINAL CAMPAIGN GOAL: $62 million

AMOUNT RAISED: $65 million

LENGTH OF CAMPAIGN: 36 months

PRESIDENT: Dr. Alphonse DeSena

BOARD CHAIR: Phillip Frick

DIRECTOR OF DEVELOPMENT: Judy Conners

CAMPAIGN HIGHLIGHT:

Exploration Place is a shining example of what a city can accomplish when everyone pulls in the same direction. The campaign to build a science and discovery center in downtown Wichita required the support of businesses and corporations, government officials and individual donors. Raising multimillion-dollar gifts across a wide spectrum of private and public donors demanded special expertise and consideration. It was an experiment in creative thinking and a successful demonstration of physics—the power of pulling together.

MISSION:

Exploration Place is a center for informal, enjoyable learning, creativity and community gathering serving residents and tourists of all ages with extraordinary resources for exploration.

HISTORY:

Dr. Alphonse DeSena was hired in 1993 to serve as Exploration Place's first president. After years of planning and preparation, fundraising and construction, Exploration Place officially opened its doors on April 1, 2000.

THE CAMPAIGN FOR EXPLORATION PLACE:

Sir Isaac Newton's first law of motion declares, in part, that "an object in motion tends to stay in motion with the same speed and in the same direction unless acted upon by an unbalanced force." In their quest to build a landmark science center along the banks of the Arkansas River, Wichita leaders and fundraisers put into motion a physics project of monumental proportions, a demonstration of *net force*—acceleration in the same direction.

Said Bob Knight, the city's mayor at the time of the campaign, "There were a lot of back-seat drivers. 'Don't get too bold. Don't dream these great, exciting dreams,' they said." But bold, innovative thinking was exactly what Wichita needed. The dream was to create a stimulating educational center that would captivate as well as motivate visitors to learn more about how the world works. Imaginative thinking and out-of-the-box creativity were not only called for—they were essential to its success.

> *"When working with public and private funding, one must recognize the need for constant communication between the institution and its donors."*
>
> —ROBERT F. HARTSOOK, JD, EdD
> CONSULTANT

The City of Wichita and a group of civic leaders had already considered the possibility of combining the city-run Omnisphere with the Children's Museum. The venture sounded very promising. A committee, chaired by Phillip Frick, studied the many facets of such an undertaking, and Dr. Alphonse DeSena was hired to head the new organization.

Said Dr. DeSena, "There was actually significant support from many Wichita corporate and philanthropic sectors, but I wondered to what extent this community could stretch to achieve a $62 million goal."

Initial fundraising efforts uncovered a powerful force in accelerating the campaign. The widow of a longtime Wichita aviation executive gave a generous lead gift of $10 million. Right on the heels of that gift followed a $20 million show of support from the Sedgwick County Commission. This private-public endorsement was typical of the wide range of funding provided for *Extraordinary Futures Start Here.*

A campaign that seeks to create a partnership between public agencies and private individuals must understand that the money is received in different ways. However, the principles of major gift fundraising remain the same.

Said counsel Bob Hartsook, "When working with public and private funding, one must recognize the need for constant communication between the institution and its donors." Just because a "donor" is a government agency does not mean there are no issues of cultivation. On the contrary, government agencies, just as with foundations and corporations, are not inanimate money-dispensing machines. They are all made up of individuals who need to be cultivated and compelled to join forces and support a campaign to "achieve greatness in their community."

The ability of Exploration Place supporters and fundraisers to involve the City in a positive, unified venture was one of Wichita's finest moments. In an unusual show of faith and boldness, city leaders—public and private—rejected naysaying and took hold of the same end of the rope.

This did not happen spontaneously. Government officials are not known for their willingness to be daring and innovative. This kind of unified support required extensive communication and constant cultivation.

In the process, the Wichita City Council agreed to allocate $1 million for property, adjust a major boulevard and donate 20 acres for the facility. The City of Wichita then provided a lease of property to Sedgwick County. The County, as owner of the building, extended a long-term agreement with Exploration Place to house its exhibits and programs. This ingenious and creative plan gave everyone a place at the table and a vested interest in seeing this venture succeed.

When it came time to recognize the generosity of supporters, the campaign leadership was advised not to overlook any gifts, whether public or private. Even support from government agencies actually reflected gifts from the people of Wichita. On numerous plaques and through exhibition sponsorships, recognition and appreciation for a wide array of support—businesses, corporations, foundations, city and county agencies, citizens and individual donors—is evident throughout the new building.

"I think the most important lesson we learned was that prospective donors want to be educated about the project. They want to know why the project is important to the community. This takes substantially more effort and time than is usually expected."

—PHILLIP FRICK
BOARD CHAIRMAN

"I think the most important lesson we learned was that prospective donors want to be educated about the project. They want to know why the project is important to the community. This takes substantially more effort and time than is usually expected," offered Chairman Frick.

Many people added their financial muscle to the project. Million-dollar gifts were not the exception in this campaign. It was not a case of everyone giving a little or even a few giving a lot. *Extraordinary Futures Start Here* was the net force of a lot of people giving extraordinarily.

RESULTS:

Exploration Place opened with more than 98,000 square feet of indoor space filled with interactive exhibits, theaters and a simulation center. Outside, an 18-hole MiniGolf course gives visitors a look at sports through the eyes of science, while Exploration Park provides a free-play area for fun and learning. Area schools take advantage of Exploration Place's excellent educational offerings. Every weekday, busloads of students arrive at the science center for field trips. Its location along the riverfront makes Exploration Place an anchor of activity for downtown businesses and helps achieve *Extraordinary Futures*—not only for visitors of all ages, but for the entire city of Wichita.

CONSULTANT'S TIPS

CONSULTANT: ROBERT F. HARTSOOK, JD, EdD

Some campaigns require support from state and city agencies as well as funding from corporations and million-dollar donors. When this is the case:

1. **It is a matter of physics.**
   Mass X Acceleration = Net Force. Get heavy-weights pulling in the same direction.

2. **You can't fight gravity, but try to avoid "balanced forces."**
   In physics "balanced forces" (e.g., gravitational, tensional, frictional, magnetic, etc.) stop or at least decrease the acceleration of motion. In a capital campaign, the same is true of naysaying, doubt and skepticism.

3. **Expand your universe.**
   Look beyond one source for major gifts. Consider private-public partnerships, creative connections and varied naming opportunities.

Iowa State University

Ames, Iowa

CAMPAIGN NAME: "Partnership for Prominence" and "Campaign Destiny"

CAMPAIGN TASK: Endowments, programming, new buildings, scholarships, newly chaired positions and general projects.

ORIGINAL CAMPAIGN GOAL:
"Partnership for Prominence," $150 million; "Campaign Destiny," $300 million

AMOUNT RAISED:
"Partnership for Prominence," $215 million; "Campaign Destiny," $458 million

LENGTH OF CAMPAIGN:
"Partnership for Prominence" (60 months); "Campaign Destiny" (60 months)

UNIVERSITY PRESIDENT: Martin Jischke

VICE PRESIDENT OF EXTERNAL AFFAIRS:
Murray Blackwelder

ISU FOUNDATION PRESIDENT: Thomas Mitchell

CAMPAIGN HIGHLIGHT:

Fundraising is replete with folklore and myth. When Murray Blackwelder arrived as Vice President of External Affairs for Iowa State University, the school was in the middle of a stalled campaign, *Partnership for Prominence*. He heard all the reasons why big money fundraising was at a standstill. Had he believed the stories and long-standing "conventional wisdom," he would have missed some million-dollar opportunities.

MISSION:

Iowa State University of Science and Technology is a public land-grant institution serving the people of Iowa, the nation and the world through its inter-related programs of instruction, research, extension and professional service. With an institutional emphasis on areas related to science and technology, the University carries out its traditional mission of discovering, developing, disseminating and preserving knowledge.

HISTORY:

Land-grant colleges were established in the mid-1800s to respond to rapid industrialization. First chartered by the Iowa General Assembly in 1858, the Iowa institution was designated the nation's first land-grant college in 1862. The school opened in 1868 as the Iowa Agricultural College and Model Farm. The name changed in 1898 to Iowa State College of Agriculture and Mechanic Arts and was renamed Iowa State University of Science and Technology in 1959.

THE CAMPAIGN FOR IOWA STATE UNIVERSITY: LESSON ONE:

The *Partnership for Prominence* campaign had a goal of $150 million, but it had paused at around $90 million in its third year. Not only had Murray Blackwelder just arrived at Iowa State, the University president was also new. There was an initial assumption that the new Vice President of External Affairs and the new President needed time to acclimate to their roles before they achieved anything really great for the University. Instead, they were able to get things moving and completed the campaign with $215 million.

One reason things progressed so swiftly was that the team involved—the ISU president, foundation president, vice president and others—was successful at raising major gifts. "In my first six months at Iowa State we managed to raise $15 million in leadership gifts," Blackwelder revealed. First crediting serendipity—a fortuitous series of events— Blackwelder is willing to admit, when pressed, that he acquired these significant leadership gifts because, well, he asked.

> "We flew out to California and met with individual prospective donors who appeared to have a strong interest in the University, as well as a qualified capacity to give large gifts. These meetings helped change the face of fundraising at Iowa State."
>
> —MURRAY BLACKWELDER
> VICE PRESIDENT OF
> EXTERNAL AFFAIRS

"We flew out to California and met with individual prospective donors who appeared to have a strong interest in the University, as well as a qualified capacity to give large gifts. These meetings helped change the face of fundraising at Iowa State," said Blackwelder.

In the process of completing *Partnership in Prominence*, he uncovered a deferred gift of $34 million. The husband was a graduate of ISU. The couple had been involved in the life of the University for decades, and there was a natural cultivation process occurring over that time.

LESSON TWO:

"The story here is that I was advised not to visit this donor," said Blackwelder. The University expected a planned gift from the elderly couple and a lot of cultivation had transpired in years past.

The fundraising folklore among longtime staff members was, "They're giving us something, so let's not rock the boat." Blackwelder had learned not to take this kind of advice as gospel. "Don't believe everything you hear." He made a decision to visit the couple and ask about their plans to give a gift to the University.

Not only did they welcome an opportunity to talk about the deferred gift assigned in their will, but when asked if it would be possible for Blackwelder to see how the will was written, they readily agreed. As it turned out, there were some technical problems with the way it was drawn up. ISU attorneys helped them make adjustments that more accurately reflected their intentions. Rather than feeling "bothered" by the visit, the couple was genuinely appreciative that the University had demonstrated interest and asked questions.

Adjustments to the will, along with the maturation of the invested monies, translated into an $80 million donation to the University—an obvious and substantial lead gift for *Campaign Destiny*. At the time this not only represented the largest gift to any Iowa public institution, but also the largest to any college of agriculture in the United States.

There are millions of dollars of missed opportunities when fundraisers buy into anecdotal advice versus pursuing their own good instincts. Said Blackwelder, "Rather than simply accepting fundraising myths about certain prospects, you can build trust among donors by being willing to make the phone call, visit face to face and ask for the gift." For Iowa State University, this was the difference between stagnation and *Destiny*.

> "Rather than simply accepting fundraising myths about certain prospects, you can build trust among donors by being willing to make the phone call, visit face to face and ask for the gift."
>
> —MURRAY BLACKWELDER
> VICE PRESIDENT OF
> EXTERNAL AFFAIRS

RESULTS:

New curricula were developed for undergraduate and graduate programs. Outright and deferred gifts funded new faculty professorships and chairs. The campaign financed more than 10 building projects. Gifts supported new construction of buildings for the College of Engineering, the College of Family and Consumer Sciences, the College of Design and the Plant Sciences Institute. *Campaign Destiny* also opened up opportunities for aid to students through scholarships, fellowships, internships and cooperative experiences. Six hundred fourteen undergraduate and graduate scholarships were created.

Consultant's Tips

Rather than buy into notions about which major donors will give and which will not, use the lessons of Iowa State University of Science and Technology to test fundraising theories.

1. Observation.
Identify donors who have a capacity to give major gifts as well as an interest in the organization.

2. Hypothesis.
Establish a specific amount of giving potential and begin to cultivate a stronger donor relationship.

3. Controlled Experiment.
Make the call. Make the visit. Ask for the gift. See for yourself.

4. Conclusion.
Assess the response and reaction from the gift. If the donor's answer is yes, the experiment was a success. If the donor's answer is maybe or a qualified no ("I have extenuating circumstances," "Not at this time," etc.), you have established a new relationship that will allow you to determine when the time is right.

Guadalupe Center, Inc.
Kansas City, Missouri

CAMPAIGN NAME: "The Guadalupe Center Capital Campaign"

CAMPAIGN TASK: To expand its existing building, add a new three-story building and increase programming in the cultural and culinary arts.

ORIGINAL CAMPAIGN GOAL: $4.9 million

AMOUNT RAISED: $5.1 million

LENGTH OF CAMPAIGN: 36 months

EXECUTIVE DIRECTOR: Cris Medina

Guadalupe Center, Inc.

Campaign Highlight:

No organization, no matter how large or how long it has been in existence, can assume that everyone understands and appreciates its mission and what it has accomplished. A non-profit should continually encourage a lifestyle of enlarging its circle of supportive volunteers. The next step in generating significant gift giving is to equip and motivate that circle of friends to get the organization's story out to individuals with an ability to give major money. Guadalupe Center not only benefited from new friends who were willing to make large gifts, but their public association with these donors brought better visibility and recognition for the organization.

Mission:

Dedicated to improving the quality of life for families through the provision of advocacy, economic enhancement, education, social services, recreation and the promotion of Latino Culture.

History:

The Guadalupe Center began in 1919. The Mexican Revolution of the early 1900s prompted an exodus of Mexican nationals who moved north. Along with new opportunities, many Mexicans faced discrimination and hardships. The Guadalupe Center became one of the nation's first social service agencies for Latinos.

THE CAMPAIGN FOR GUADALUPE CENTER, INC.:

"Every nonprofit and its leadership is called to action—increasing visibility and relationship building—for the organization," said consultant Eric Staley. Clearly, some organizations are more willing than others to commit themselves to the work of major gift fundraising. The Guadalupe Center's success was testimony to the fact that its executive director, Cris Medina—along with staff, board and volunteers—made a decisive choice to do what needed to be done for a successful capital campaign.

As its first major campaign and one of the first ever for a Latino-based agency, Guadalupe Center's decision set a powerful precedent for the Hispanic community. The leadership of Guadalupe Center took the advice of their consultant to clarify and focus on the mission, identify additional people who cared about the organization and increase Guadalupe Center's visibility, particularly among people who had the potential for making significant gifts.

> "I went to all the solicitations, but without an introduction from members of our steering committee, most of those calls would not have happened. I would tell people, 'If you can get me in there, I can present our case.'"
>
> —CRIS MEDINA
> EXECUTIVE DIRECTOR

The role of a consultant is always to help clients re-evaluate and clarify the mission and keep them focused. At times, a fundraising consultant must be willing to play the devil's advocate, asking the tough questions: "How many clients do you serve?" "How successful are you at providing services?"

"What changes are really being accomplished in people's lives?" "Does the community really know what you do and what is accomplished inside this building?"

Even though Guadalupe Center had a circle of friends who cared about the institution, it was challenged by its consultant to make sure everyone was on the same page before launching into the campaign. Staley's questions and prodding revealed that even some board members and volunteers were not fully aware of the Center's accomplishments and scope of mission.

The risk of not addressing these issues head-on is that, without this accurate perspective, even those closest to the organization can make wrong assumptions. Some of these decisions will, at the least, be unproductive, even counterproductive to the future of the organization. Said Staley, "Without that deliberate exercise of drawing this information out of a leadership team, they are not really in a position yet to go out and ask for major gifts."

In addition, every campaign needs supporters who will put their reputations on the line and associate themselves with the organization in a very personal way. It is a powerful thing when someone who has already made a large gift will say—boldly, confidently and sincerely—"This is a great group that deserves the most generous financial gift you can muster!"

This kind of self-promotion was initially culturally uncomfortable for Guadalupe Center. As it does for many groups, "getting the story out" felt too much like bragging. It was a mindset those associated with Guadalupe Center had to adjust in order to ask for major gifts. Once they understood the importance and necessity, many were anxious to tell the community about the Center's wonderful work. This willingness to go out and raise the visibility of the organization created a contagious enthusiasm.

Steering committee members were active in opening doors to potential donors. Said Medina, "I went to all the solicitations, but without an introduction from members of our steering committee, most of those calls would not have happened. I would tell people, 'If you can get me in there, I can present our case.'"

Supporters stepped in and added their names and network of relationships to the campaign. This elevated credibility and opened the door for Medina and other Guadalupe Center representatives to ask for large gifts.

Said Medina, "This campaign has really increased our visibility. Now there is not one major foundation in the Kansas City area that doesn't know we're here. We brought many people out to see the work we do. Most had never been here before the campaign. After 20 years of service to the community, we are now empowered to give people an even greater opportunity to grow and develop."

> "This campaign has really increased our visibility. Now there is not one major foundation in the Kansas City area that doesn't know we're here."
>
> —CRIS MEDINA
> EXECUTIVE DIRECTOR

RESULTS:

The Guadalupe Center's new building is 24,000 square feet and houses five of its 14 programs. The building includes an art gallery and a 200-seat, state-of-the-art theater with an indoor and outdoor stage. The culinary arts wing of the expansion has two major components: a food preparation vocational training facility and a nonprofit catering service.

CONSULTANT'S TIPS

CONSULTANT: R. ERIC STALEY, PhD

Increasing the visibility of an organization is more than "horn blowing." It is a chance to connect with businesses, corporations and individuals not only willing to offer strong financial support, but to come along as new friends.

1. **Get everyone on the same page.**
   Revisit and clarify the organization's mission.

2. **Talk to everyone.**
   Be willing to go outside the normal parameters of support.

3. **Invite everyone.**
   Bring together a circle of friends—old and new—who are willing to boast about the organization's accomplishments.

4. **Ask everyone ...**
   Who has an interest and the ability to give major money.

CHAPTER SIX

EXPAND YOUR OPPORTUNITY

"The number one car driven by millionaires in America today is a Ford pickup truck."

—Thomas J. Stanley
"The Millionaire Next Door"

Boys & Girls Club of McAlester

McAlester, Oklahoma

CAMPAIGN NAME: "Catch the Vision"

CAMPAIGN TASK: To build a new 41,000-square-foot, multipurpose field house with basketball courts, indoor batting cages, indoor soccer and space for specialized teen programs.

ORIGINAL CAMPAIGN GOAL: $2.5 million

AMOUNT RAISED: $2.7 million

LENGTH OF CAMPAIGN: 30 months

EXECUTIVE DIRECTOR: Chris Martin

CAMPAIGN HIGHLIGHT:

Virtually every organization starts out underestimating the potential for major gifts in its community. Whether it is a small town in eastern Oklahoma or a big city in Missouri, just about everyone says, "You just can't raise that kind of money in this town." The difference between an organization that overcomes this roadblock versus one that camps on the side of skepticism is an openness to new ideas, a commitment to learning new things and a willingness to do what needs to be done.

MISSION:

The purpose of the Boys & Girls Club of McAlester, Inc. is to assure and enhance the quality of life for all boys and girls regardless of race, color or creed by providing programs that build character and life skills. The Boys & Girls Club of McAlester recognizes that all youth deserve a chance for personal growth, with access to basic living experiences as well as basic skills in sports development. In order to direct their abundant energies in constructive directions, the Boys & Girls Club provides services that develop the physical and mental health of the youth in our charge.

HISTORY:

Boys & Girls Clubs of America began in Hartford, Connecticut in 1860 as the Boys Club. In 1990 the national organization was changed to Boys & Girls Clubs of America. The Boys Club of McAlester began in 1960. The Girls Club of McAlester began two years later. The two groups merged in 1992 to form today's Boys & Girls Club of McAlester.

THE CAMPAIGN FOR BOYS & GIRLS CLUB OF MCALESTER:

During this campaign, as with all campaigns, it was very important for campaign committee members and volunteers to grasp the realities and concepts of major gift fundraising. Before things could get in full swing, consultant Robert Swanson went over the classic obstacles and textbook fundraising lessons. Because of the determination of campaign committee members and volunteers to learn how fundraising really works and to apply those lessons, the Boys & Girls Club of McAlester managed to exchange old ideas about philanthropy for new donors and great gifts.

"What I was really looking for—along with a capacity to give a large gift—was a strong association and commitment to the organization."

—ROBERT G. SWANSON
CONSULTANT

One of the first obstacles to overcome was the unfamiliarity in asking for or making large stretch gifts. Initially, this was a huge concept to accept. "I explained that in order for the board and volunteers to go out and ask for major gifts, they would have to lead the way with their own stretch gifts," said Swanson. "These were people who truly believed in the importance of the organization, but many of them were still in their 30s and 40s. Giving a $10,000 gift over a three-year period really challenged their thinking about fundraising."

During the assessment process, a board member was identified who had the capacity to give a significant lead gift to the campaign. "What I was really looking for—along with a capacity to give a large gift—was a strong association and commitment to the organization," said Swanson. This donor had both.

The board was advised to approach this board member for a $300,000 challenge gift, and was encouraged to ask, "If the board gives $300,000 (which was going to be a stretch), would you be willing to provide a match dollar for dollar?"

This is where the rubber met the road. Board members could have said what they already "knew" to be true, "We can't ask someone in little McAlester, Oklahoma for $300,000, and we certainly don't have another $300,000 of giving on our board." Instead, they chose to suspend their disbelief and go with expert opinion. "They gulped," said Swanson, "but they did it. At first they wondered, 'Maybe he could give $300,000 over a five-year period, but can we really ask him for an immediate matching gift?'" Encouraged to go ahead and ask, the board was rewarded by his acceptance, which created great initial energy for the campaign.

Not only did the board meet the challenge, but it secured well over $300,000 from its members, bringing the total of this lead challenge to $640,000—a quarter of the total campaign goal.

When the board of directors first set a $2.5 million goal for *Catch a Vision*, everyone understood this would be a challenge for a town of 18,000. The difference between this organization and others was that its board was ready to try something new, develop a good fundraising plan and stick to the plan.

Said Executive Director Chris Martin, "At first, asking for big gifts was a challenge, but we learned to do it. When we remembered why we were asking—for the boys and girls—it was easier than many of us thought it might be. I've spent a lot of years with the Club, and it was very satisfying to see people respond to the need."

Said Board President Steve Brock, "The staff members at the Club realize the critical role they play. You can see it in the kids' faces when they walk through the door after school. It's truly a mentoring relationship." It was this commitment to securing a safe and structured environment that kept the Club moving toward its fundraising goals—even when it meant trying new things and asking for big gifts.

"Sometimes you just have to be simple-minded enough to take direction," said Martin. "We learned to take the guidance and counsel. It worked for us. Come to McAlester, and you can see the results."

> *"Sometimes you just have to be simple-minded enough to take direction. We learned to take the guidance and counsel. It worked for us."*
>
> —CHRIS MARTIN
> EXECUTIVE DIRECTOR

RESULTS:

McAlester's new athletic complex provides children with a place where they can enjoy themselves free from the onslaught of negative peer pressure. The Club is a safe haven where children and teens can learn and play in a fun, structured and supervised environment. The new facility has six basketball courts for practice, games, tournaments and special events. It also includes indoor batting cages, indoor soccer areas and specialized teen programs.

CONSULTANT'S TIPS
CONSULTANT: ROBERT G. SWANSON

Nearly every nonprofit wrestles with its ability to raise big gifts. It is essential for an organization to overcome this barrier and move on to the important business of fundraising.

1. Listen to the experts.
Seasoned fundraisers will tell you money is available if the cause is compelling—but you have to make your case to the right people.

2. Stay open to new ideas.
Smart fundraisers understand that nobody wants to give money away—but donors are always interested in making a real and lasting difference in people's lives. This is an important new lesson organizations must learn before undertaking a campaign.

3. Do the work.
Major gift fundraising requires a lot of research, phone calls, face-to-face meetings with prospects and intentional, well-prepared solicitations—but it is worth it.

Trading in a tired cliche ("We can't raise that kind of money in this town.") for tried and true fundraising strategies is the first step in achieving a successful campaign.

Dyck Arboretum of the Plains

Hesston, Kansas

CAMPAIGN NAME: "Enhancing Excellence"

CAMPAIGN TASK: To build a 3,700-square-foot Visitor and Education Center and enhance programming.

ORIGINAL CAMPAIGN GOAL: $685,000

AMOUNT RAISED: $685,000 plus

LENGTH OF CAMPAIGN: 30 months

EXECUTIVE DIRECTOR: Larry Vickerman

Campaign Highlight:

Persistence and tenacity were the hallmarks of this campaign. The executive director went to great lengths to keep potential donors informed of the campaign's progress. His diligence in doing so yielded impressive results. The Arboretum's *Enhancing Excellence* campaign generated gifts that never would have been realized without a relentless commitment to donor cultivation.

Mission:

The Dyck Arboretum, a prairie garden, exists to educate people about the benefits of appreciating, preserving and utilizing native and adaptable plants.

History:

Harold and Elva Mae Dyck began the Arboretum in 1981 by donating property and establishing a $7 million endowment to provide for continued care of the acreage, transforming it from a former wheat field into a lovely and lavish prairie garden.

THE CAMPAIGN FOR DYCK ARBORETUM OF THE PLAINS:

For more than 20 years, the Dyck Arboretum of the Plains has offered visitors and students educational programs focusing on plant physiology and reproduction, plant adaptations, horticulture, the significance of Kansas natural heritage and the preservation of habitat for wildlife.

Year after year, interest in these programs, as well as an increase in numbers of visitors, created a demand for an indoor facility to house program staff and create a venue for year-round events and activities.

A campaign to build a Visitor and Education Center was the Arboretum's first attempt at major gift fundraising. Its executive director at the time had never been part of a capital campaign, but his commitment to the project made up for the learning curve that comes with raising large gifts.

> *"One reason individuals, businesses and foundations were so willing to get behind the project was because they could see that things were moving along at a steady, even accelerating clip."*
>
> —LARRY VICKERMAN
> EXECUTIVE DIRECTOR

As a separate organization, but closely affiliated with Hesston College, the Arboretum worked in cooperation with the school's ongoing campaign, *Enhancing Excellence.*

Despite the city's strong support, with a population of less than 4,000, it was imperative for the Arboretum to look beyond Hesston's borders for major gifts.

Said Executive Director Larry Vickerman, "While we had good backing from the town of Hesston—its leaders and its populace—practically, we needed to look at a wider giving area. The city was also supporting other ventures, and we agreed that many Kansas communities and organizations would be interested in seeing this project succeed."

Early in the campaign the Arboretum received a Kansas Community Service Tax Credit for $100,000. Since the organization is located in a smaller rural community, the program allowed area businesses and individuals an amazing 70 percent income tax credit.

Although tax credits are not always easy to dispense, through persistence and hard work the Arboretum not only made use of the entire $100,000, but later in the campaign received an additional $100,000 tax credit. The Arboretum managed to allocate this second gift throughout the Hesston community as well as surrounding cities in less than six months.

The Arboretum's executive director was tireless in writing grants to numerous foundations around the country. "We would write the grant and send it over to our consultant for review," said Vickerman. Added consultant Bob Hartsook, "Larry demonstrated the importance of persistence in creating new gifts for the organization."

Vickerman's notes and letters to the executive directors of various foundations were never overaggressive, but, in time, people receiving his consistent and informative communiques could have no doubt that he was serious about receiving major gifts from their foundations.

Just months into the campaign, the Arboretum received its first outright grant given by the Stanley Smith Horticultural Trust out of Berkeley, California. A gift from the Wichita-Greyhound Charities, Inc. Foundation followed.

A cash contribution and in-kind gift of services—water, sewer, gas, and so on—from the town of Hesston, authorized by the City Council, provided a significant gift for the campaign.

Seeds of hard work planted months and months before began to take root and produce fruit. Grant acceptances came from the Western Resources Foundation, the James S. and John L. Knight Foundation, and a second gift from the Wichita-Greyhound Charities, Inc. Foundation.

Said Vickerman, "One reason individuals, businesses and foundations were so willing to get behind the project was because they could see that things were moving along at a steady, even accelerating clip."

A spectacular gift from the J.E. and L.E. Mabee Foundation for more than $100,000 took *Enhancing Excellence* within range of its goal.

> "When we got within $50,000 of our goal, I made a call to check up on the Lied grant. They had shown some interest over the summer so the call let them know that their gift would put us over the top."
>
> —LARRY VICKERMAN
> EXECUTIVE DIRECTOR

One gift, in particular, illustrates the power of persistence and the importance of constant communication with prospective donors. Vickerman explained, "We'd written a grant to the Lied Foundation Trust asking for $50,000. At the time, we felt as though it might be a bit of a long shot, but now we were just that far away from our goal."

Despite the fact that the Lied Foundation was out of state, and even with a slim chance of receiving a gift, Vickerman stayed in contact with the foundation's executive director by letter. Always polite, always chronicling the progress of the campaign and the accomplishments and goals of the organization, Vickerman kept up the one-way conversation as long as there was still a possibility of receiving a gift. The fundraising rule of thumb, "If they haven't said no, there's still an opportunity to cultivate a major gift."

Said Vickerman, "When we got within $50,000 of our goal, I made a call to check up on the Lied grant. They had shown some interest over the summer so the call let them know that their gift would put us over the top." After a week of phone calls back and forth, answering questions and keeping the conversation going, the Lied Foundation agreed to accept the grant and donate the entire $50,000 to the Arboretum project.

"It was a great way to finish off the campaign," Vickerman reminisced. Determination and good cultivation instincts took moderate soil—long shots and small-town resources— and raised a garden of lavish, major gifts.

RESULTS:

The beautiful limestone and cedar Visitor and Education Center provides an added venue for education as well as recreation and entertainment. A year-round lecture series features information on horticulture, natural science and the arts. Visitors can now enjoy picturesque settings outdoors, as well as rent the facility for reunions, birthday and anniversary celebrations, graduations, wedding receptions and other special events. Along with the Arboretum, the Visitor and Education Center is used by Hesston College to enhance its educational programs.

CONSULTANT'S TIPS

CONSULTANT: ROBERT F. HARTSOOK, JD, EdD

The word "cultivation" is closely associated with agriculture. The principles of cultivation are so relevant to enriching donor relationships that it has become standard fundraising jargon. Take these tips from the "cultivation experts" at the Dyck Arboretum of the Plains.

1. **No two situations have the same cultivation (soil) conditions.**
   Different donors require different levels and varieties of cultivation. Donors living out of state may require something different than local donors.

2. **Start with the basics: light, water and temperature.**
   Donors need to be enlightened on the accomplishments of the organization and the progress of the campaign. Irrigate with good communication. Make sure donor relationships do not grow cold.

3. **Check the soil.**
   Some donor relationships are harder to cultivate than others. Some are naturally more productive, while others need work to remove rocky issues. Be intentional and persistent about turning the soil of donor relationships into healthy fields for cultivation.

4. **Ask the experts.**
   Find out which organizations and causes prospective donors have supported in the past. Do research to uncover their interests and passions. Just as there are local extension offices for testing plants and soil, there are smart ways to identify and cultivate prospective donors.

Girl Scout Council of The Ozark Area

Joplin, Missouri

CAMPAIGN NAME: "Building Tomorrow …
  Girl by Girl"

Campaign Task: To initiate new programming and make improvements to the 50-year-old aging infrastructures and facilities at the Ozark Girl Scout camp. Additions to the camp included a new activity lodge, a camp challenge course with rappelling tower, and an education and service center with administrative offices and computer lab, as well as an endowment for building maintenance.

ORIGINAL CAMPAIGN GOAL: $2.2 million

AMOUNT RAISED: $2.2 million plus

LENGTH OF CAMPAIGN: 36 months

EXECUTIVE DIRECTOR: Karen Morgan

DIRECTOR OF DEVELOPMENT: Tiffany Brooks

GIRL SCOUT COUNCIL OF THE OZARK AREA

THE CAMPAIGN FOR GIRL SCOUT COUNCIL OF THE OZARK AREA:

Before *Building Tomorrow ... Girl by Girl*, GSCOA had never attempted a capital campaign. The Council was working hard to enhance visibility and increase its work among girls not typically served by Girl Scouts. A new emphasis on under-served populations—girls in rural and poorer areas, those in nontraditional settings and girls without strong parental support—generated a need for major fundraising to support increased capacity.

> *"Someone must keep a finger on the pulse of the many important and often tedious issues of an Integrated Fundraising Campaign[SM]."*
>
> —ROBERT G. SWANSON
> CONSULTANT

Because of their needs, GSCOA was encouraged to implement an Integrated Fundraising Campaign[SM], a campaign to raise capital and endowment dollars while maintaining or growing the annual fund. It was important to ensure that the administration of the campaign would be seamless, particularly since this was the Council's first campaign.

"At our consultant's recommendation," said Executive Director Karen Morgan, "we first hired an additional person to assist with annual giving and to help with communications during the campaign. Anticipating this additional need, and addressing it before it became a crisis, helped in practical ways. It also helped sustain morale and energy while the agency juggled two important fundraising ventures." Added consultant Robert Swanson, "Someone must keep a finger on the pulse of the many important, and often tedious, issues of an Integrated Fundraising Campaign[SM]."

One of the most important aspects of administrating the campaign was a commitment to staying in constant contact with longtime supporters and prospective donors. Communication was a linchpin issue for this campaign. Said Swanson, "Whether it is a staff person or a volunteer, some-one needs to be 'Information Central' for a campaign. For this campaign, that person was Tiffany Brooks."

Said Brooks, "We were encouraged to start a monthly newsletter to build interest in the campaign among prospects. The "First Monday Memo" was also helpful in keeping donors aware of our progress. One thing I personally learned from the campaign was the importance of staying in touch with potential donors. Gifts that we thought were impossible came through after months of sending updates and personal notes." Brooks' consistent communication with prospects and donors proved indispensable to the campaign's success.

Several foundation gifts and grant options created extraordinary opportunities, but they also generated more detail-laden work. Everyone played a part in garnering these gifts: a J.E. and L.E. Mabee Foundation grant of $200,000, a $25,000 gift from the C.W. Titus Foundation, a Kemper Foundation gift of $15,000, and $250,000 in state tax credits (GSCOA was the only agency in Joplin to get state tax credits that year). However, it took one person looking over all the details and timing of the process to make sure everything was done right.

While this should be the norm for every campaign, unfortunately it is not always the case. One unreturned call, one late grant application, one overlooked prospect can translate into multimillion-dollar mistakes.

Having a person who is vigilant about following up on the details, answering donor questions and communicating faithfully with volunteers can make the difference between a good effort and a truly great campaign.

Results:

Camp additions, including a new activity lodge, a camp challenge course with rappelling tower, and an education and service center with administrative offices and computer lab give the Council a boost in reaching more girls. At the dedication ceremony for the Education and Service Center for Girls, the Girl Scouts of the USA National Executive Director Marsha Johnson Evans acknowledged the Council's overwhelming success, "You are a pacesetter Council for the nation." The new Center, along with camp improvements and additions, has substantially increased the opportunities available for disadvantaged girls in the Ozark Area.

> *"One thing I personally learned from the campaign was the importance of staying in touch with potential donors. Gifts that we thought were impossible came through after months of sending updates and personal notes."*
>
> —Tiffany Brooks
> Director of Development

Consultant's Tips

Consultants: R. Eric Staley, PhD
& Robert G. Swanson

Make sure someone is designated or can serve as a clearinghouse for information.

1. The devil is in the details.

It is important to have a point-person who knows when the grant proposals are due, which donors are waiting for a question to be answered, where the campaign stands in dollars raised—essentially everything.

2. Get someone who is both detail-oriented and people-oriented.

Not everyone who is strong administratively is also good with people. Not every person who is likable and responsive to people is able to stay focused on the details. Donors will expect to deal with someone who is both—accurate and amiable.

3. Keep the gatekeeper informed.

Since this will be a go-to person for information, it is important to pass along anything new or unusual. Campaigns require everyone involved to follow through on assigned tasks, but having at least one person who makes it his or her business to cross all the "t's" and dot all the "i's" will make for a smoother process, happier donors and a more successful campaign.

Sunflower House

Shawnee, Kansas

CAMPAIGN NAME: "A Promise to Protect"

CAMPAIGN TASK: To purchase land; construct a new, child-friendly facility; enhance programming; and build an endowment.

ORIGINAL CAMPAIGN GOAL: $4.25 million

AMOUNT RAISED: $4.3 million

LENGTH OF CAMPAIGN: 30 months

EXECUTIVE DIRECTOR: Brenda Sharpe

DIRECTOR OF DEVELOPMENT: Michelle Lawrence

CAMPAIGN HIGHLIGHT:

Some organizations are more naturally in tune with making a case for support. Sunflower House was a perfect example of what it means to believe in the organization's mission. This campaign team was exceptional at doing its homework before each and every solicitation. When it came to making a case for support, team members had absolutely no fear.

MISSION:

To prevent child abuse and neglect in the Greater Kansas City community through child-centered programs and interventions.

HISTORY:

Sunflower House was the result of a successful merger in 1997 between the Child Abuse Prevention Coalition, founded in 1977, and the Sunflower Children's Center, founded in 1994.

THE CAMPAIGN FOR SUNFLOWER HOUSE:

"Making a positive difference in the lives of others is the foundation of any campaign," consultant Robert Swanson said. "This was a textbook campaign from a technical standpoint. But it was the passion and professionalism of staff and volunteer leadership that drove the campaign to success."

A big reason why Sunflower House was able to cultivate and solicit prospects so successfully was because they believed so strongly in the case for support. They were able to share, one-on-one, a powerful message for helping the most vulnerable members of society. As a result, they brought hundreds of new supporters—hopefully, lifetime supporters—to their fight against child abuse.

> *"We learned there is a right and wrong way to conduct a campaign."*
>
> —MARK PARKINSON
> CAMPAIGN CO-CHAIR

During one meeting with the J.E. and L.E. Mabee Foundation, Sunflower House co-chairs and Executive Director Brenda Sharpe demonstrated their boldness and confidence in the organization. "We had an 'ask' figure in mind," Sharpe said, "but the meeting was going so well that we felt confident enough to increase it to $450,000. We had learned by this point that prospective donors can always say no, but if it's an appropriate amount, you might as well ask."

Fact-finding, strategic planning and extensive discussion and research are hard work, but, when done beforehand, give the board members, volunteers and staff the confidence they need to walk into a solicitation meeting and make an articulate, passionate case for support.

179

Sunflower House enjoyed a tremendous solicitation success rate. Of the approximately 300 gifts solicited during the campaign, only two were turned down. The key to this success: passion for the mission, preparation before the solicitation and diligent follow-up afterward.

"We learned there is a right and wrong way to conduct a campaign," said Co-Chair Mark Parkinson. "There's a methodical process, and each step must be accomplished in turn. You need a great organization with great leaders, a supportive board and cultivated relationships in the philanthropic community. You can't just call a foundation without developing a relationship."

Everyone associated with *A Promise to Protect* understood that the campaign was not about a building. It was about protecting children. To most of us, the idea that someone might intentionally hurt a child is unfathomable. Fortunately, for children who are victims of abuse, the Sunflower House is one place where they can find the safety and protection of adults who have their best interests at heart.

For the Sunflower House staff, board members and volunteers, solicitations were never something to be feared. They were one more wonderful opportunity to garner support for the mission—another way of fulfilling *A Promise to Protect*.

RESULTS:

A building designed for the safety and security of children provides young victims with an environment for dealing with the realities and aftermath of abuse. Years ago, victims had to make a formal disclosure of abuse as many as seven different times to different people in a wide variety of locations: social-service agencies, police departments, medical facilities, etc. These stressful investigations tended to confuse children; the result was conflicting testimony and alleged abusers walking free. The new building creates a comfortable and safe environment that encourages children to open up and let the truth tumble out.

"We had an 'ask' figure in mind, but the meeting was going so well that we felt confident enough to increase it to $450,000. We had learned by this point that prospective donors can always say no, but if it's an appropriate amount, you might as well ask."

—BRENDA SHARPE
EXECUTIVE DIRECTOR

CONSULTANT'S TIPS
CONSULTANT: ROBERT G. SWANSON

Just because an organization has a compelling mission and a strong case for support does not mean board members and volunteers "own" the message.

1. **Assess enthusiasm and support.**
   Be honest about the level of commitment and enthusiasm board members and volunteers have for the organization and campaign.

2. **Make a clear and compelling case.**
   Make sure everyone understands why you are undertaking a campaign. Remember, it is not for a building; it is for what is going on inside the building. It is not for programming; it is for what the programming will do in people's lives. It is not for an endowment; it is to ensure that the organization will be there to help others in the future.

3. **Solicit gifts only after No. 1 and No. 2 are nailed down.**
   It is much easier to get board members and volunteers motivated to make calls and visits, and solicit gifts when they are completely confident of the message. Even if they make attempts, unless they really believe what they are saying they will only be going through the motions rather than delivering a compelling message for support. This will be reflected in the quantity and quality of gifts received.

The Nelson-Atkins Museum of Art

Kansas City, Missouri

CAMPAIGN NAME: "Generations: A Gift To Us—
A Gift From Us"

CAMPAIGN TASK: To undertake a major facility
expansion, conduct renovations, enhance programming and establish an endowment.

ORIGINAL CAMPAIGN GOAL: $125 million

AMOUNT RAISED: $200 million plus

LENGTH OF CAMPAIGN: 36 months

DIRECTOR: Marc F. Wilson

Campaign Highlight:

Not every campaign calls for a committee of luminaries. But when you set out to raise hundreds of millions of dollars for a landmark museum, it doesn't hurt. What made the Nelson-Atkins Museum of Art's committee so special, however, was not the level of visibility of its players, but the deep-seated dedication each one held for the Museum and for this campaign.

Mission:

Dedicated to the enjoyment and understanding of the visual arts and the varied cultures they represent. It is committed through its collections and programs to being a vital partner in the educational and cultural life of Kansas City and a pre-eminent institution both nationally and internationally. It strives to achieve this goal by adherence to the highest professional standards in the collection, preservation, exhibition and interpretation of works of art.

History:

When William Rockhill Nelson died in 1915, his will included a proviso that, following the death of his wife and daughter, all of the remaining proceeds from his estate should be allocated for "the purchase of works of art and reproductions of works of the fine arts, such as paintings, engravings, sculpture, tapestries and rare books ... which will contribute to the delectation and enjoyment of the public generally." A museum was eventually built in 1933 from monies supplied by the Nelson family and friends, as well as an estate gift left by Mary Atkins, a former schoolteacher who willed $300,000 to Kansas City for the founding of an art museum.

THE CAMPAIGN FOR THE NELSON-ATKINS MUSEUM OF ART:

Some exceptionally committed and well-known Kansas City supporters were at the helm of this campaign—Hall, Sosland, Bloch. Name recognition certainly gave *Generations* an edge out of the gate, but even a high-profile board will stall if there is insufficient energy and enthusiasm. Said counsel Eric Staley, "I will always look at this leadership team as the best example of the fact that a dedicated leadership—and I emphasize 'dedicated'—moves the success of a campaign from a question of 'if' to the much more exciting question of 'when.'"

Generations offers a case study in how a traditional campaign structure allows a major campaign to flex and succeed. "This was a campaign of magnificent leadership enabled by a precise and well-planned vision," said Staley.

> "I will always look at this leadership team as the best example of the fact that a dedicated leadership—and I emphasize 'dedicated'—moves the success of a campaign from a question of 'if' to the much more exciting question of 'when.'"
>
> —R. ERIC STALEY, PhD
> CONSULTANT

Seven decades of art audiences had enjoyed The Nelson-Atkins Museum of Art. In that time, the Museum's collections had grown significantly. Everyone agreed that more room was needed to display important works of art being kept in storage for lack of gallery space. Reference and research capabilities had fallen short of demand, programming outpaced space, and parking was wholly insufficient. A major campaign was in order.

"It is easy to understand how a campaign chaired by Adele Hall and Morton Sosland would have a high probability for success," said Staley. "But until one has an opportunity to work with these two extraordinary people, it is impossible to understand the true meaning of dedication. Adele and Morton had fire in the belly from Day One to the close of the campaign, and they made the goals of the campaign come to life in the absence of architectural visualizations. Moreover, they motivated and set the standards for all the other volunteers down the line, whose accomplishments were equally amazing across the board. The leadership was, in a word, inspired."

While the majority of generosity for this campaign came directly from trustees and committee members, the Kansas City community was supportive of the effort. Corporate gifts also demonstrated a respect for the Nelson-Atkins' past and a strong belief in its future. In all, more than 4,000 donors made the campaign successful.

Generations was the largest private-dollar campaign in the history of Kansas City at that time, and one of the largest museum campaigns in the country (others include the Museum of Fine Arts—Boston, and the Museum of Modern Art and the Metropolitan Museum, both in New York City). Extraordinarily, all but approximately $6 million was raised locally, and deferred gifts amounted to less than 10 percent of the $200-plus million raised.

Results:

Expansion of the Museum increased the Nelson-Atkins' size—adding 145,000 square feet of space to the existing 234,000-square-foot Museum—and enlarged its capacity to bring art appreciation and education to a new generation. Modern, contemporary and African art and photography that had been tucked away in storage can now be displayed for the pleasure of grateful art devotees. Renovations and additions also include a Museum library boasting more than 125,000 volumes for referencing, as well as meeting rooms, classrooms, bookstore, café and space for special exhibitions. A substantial endowment rounds out the benefit to The Nelson-Atkins Museum of Art from generations of donors.

"It is easy to understand how a campaign chaired by Adele Hall and Morton Sosland would have a high probability for success. But until one has an opportunity to work with these two extraordinary people, it is impossible to understand the true meaning of dedication."

—R. Eric Staley, PhD
Consultant

CONSULTANT'S TIPS
CONSULTANT: R. ERIC STALEY, PhD

Not every campaign demands a star-studded steering committee. High-profile names do not necessarily translate into a multimillion-dollar campaign. (But they can't hurt.)

1. **Build a committee of dedicated supporters.**
   When assembling a quality steering committee, look for an intensity of commitment to the mission of the organization.

2. **Encourage public association.**
   Enjoin people who care deeply about the campaign's success—people who will be more than willing to lend their names to the list of dedicated donors.

3. **Engage proven leaders.**
   And, if those names ring a bell in the community, all the better!

4. **Never forget that dedication is the real name of the game.**
   The reason *Generations* enjoyed such enormous success was because the individuals who led this campaign were highly motivated in the first place. That they were high-profile, name-brand citizens was an important, not-to-be-underestimated bonus, but a genuine dedication to the Museum was the first and greatest gift they brought to the table.

CONCLUSION

YOU ARE NOT ALONE

"Dig the well before you get thirsty."

—Harvey Mackay

Concluding Chapter—
The Capstone

Where will your nonprofit be this time next year? Are you facing immediate fiscal challenges, or do you have nagging concerns about the longevity of current funding sources? Are you limiting programs and services due to inadequate space or outdated technology? Is there more that needs to be done, but due to financial hurdles the big dreams keep getting pushed to the back burner in lieu of more urgent operational priorities?

You are not alone. As you have already read (if you journeyed through this book from cover to cover), or as you will soon see (if you jumped to the last chapter to discover how the story ends), nonprofits of all shapes and sizes face similar obstacles and opportunities.

In considering your organization's upcoming objectives, I can promise you one thing: Next year will come. Whether your group identifies and meets its challenges head on or takes advantage of the opportunities that come your way, next year will arrive right on time.

Will you be in the same place, asking the same questions, facing the same perennial issues and concerns? Or are you ready for some of the most productive, life-changing seasons your organization has ever known?

THE CAPSTONE

It is our hope that you will gather the lessons from dozens of campaigns to gain greater insights and new perspectives, moving you closer to the answers you need, in order to achieve the financial success your organization deserves.

After personally witnessing hundreds of campaigns and hearing about thousands more—coast to coast, in small towns and big cities, conducted by name-brand nonprofits and little-known agencies—I can attest to the fact that money is not in short supply. Money is always available. Wealth is virtually unlimited. Generosity is still abundant and obtainable.

I am equally confident that no one wants to give that money away—not to your organization, not to the organization next door, not to anyone. No one—not even a person of unlimited wealth or copious generosity—is interested in handing money over indiscriminately.

However, tens of thousands of individuals, foundations and corporations are still very interested in generating real-life results in the world. How interested are you in meeting these people, getting to know them, conveying your organization's story in a thoughtful, compelling way and soliciting a major gift?

Whether a nonprofit is successful in identifying the right people, making the right connections and asking for the right amount of money under the right set of circumstances is what separates a struggling "501(c)anything" with one that is well-funded.

After reading this book, you are now in a better position to reject common rationales and excuses perpetuated by multitudes of nonprofits ("There isn't enough money in our community to sustain a capital campaign," "All we need to do is mail a solicitation letter to a few thousand people," "Can't we just raffle something bigger next year?"). Instead, you have read how everyday, ordinary groups can accomplish extraordinary things by implementing smart, proven fundraising strategies.

When it comes to raising money, the only true confidence builder is proven success—raising money. And a track record of success only comes from doing the right thing. By reading this book, you now have the luxury of "experiencing" many campaigns of various sizes and sectors from conception to capstone.

In a very real way, your level of expertise has increased page by page. You have absorbed a lifetime of campaign lessons in a matter of hours. How great is that? By listening to the stories of others, you are in a better position to recognize the textbook pitfalls and reap the magnificent benefits of a major-gift campaign.

What defines a successful campaign? One word: Results! Is the organization in a stronger financial position overall following the campaign? Have all the goals—capital, operations, programming or endowment—been adequately met? Has the donor base increased? Have additional major-gift donors been added to the organization's circle of friends? Has the organization's visibility in the community been improved?

THE CAPSTONE

What will it take to achieve results for your organization? After reading this book, you will likely recognize the key ingredients:

R—Reject myths and misconceptions about major-gift fundraising.

E—Embrace smart strategies for raising big gifts.

S—Stay focused on the organization's mission.

U—Understand that no one wants to give money away.

L—Let prospects see the difference their gifts will make.

T—Tell donors how much they and their gifts are appreciated.

S—Solicit prospects who care deeply about the organization and its mission.

When we first began this journey together, I introduced *On the Money!* as a collection of simple stories that abridge and, at times, belie the complexity of major-gift fundraising. These stories are not at all meant to downplay the monumental effort and energy that goes into a campaign. They are intended to encapsulate years of hard work and extract a lesson or two that you can immediately apply to your fundraising goals.

Whether your organization's mission is to inspire youth or give sustenance to the elderly, bring renowned artists to your city or send low-income children to camp in the country, educate or entertain, assist or defend, there is one common denominator among them all—a need for money to achieve worthy goals.

The Capstone

At first glance, raising money may not appear as noble a task as ladling soup or delivering groceries, less gallant than teaching children to read or archiving a collection of priceless art. But make no mistake. The work of fundraising plays an essential and honorable role in the life of a nonprofit.

Fundraisers who truly care about the work of an organization and who are willing to learn the best practices of raising major gifts can make all the difference in the quantity and quality of services a nonprofit can provide.

Your decision to read this book reflects a vested interest in your organization. You care about its reputation in the community, its financial outlook for the future and its ability to fulfill an important mission. We do, too. Our company has always measured success by the financial and organizational success of our clients.

Where will your nonprofit be this time next year? Wherever you are, it is our sincere wish that you and your organization will in every way be right "On the Money!"

Contributors

Matthew J. Beem, CFRE
President, Hartsook Essential
"Fundraisers are the conduit between people's desires to become part of something greater than themselves and the opportunities that exist in society to do so. Philanthropy is first about helping people. It's human and emotional."

Murray Blackwelder
Executive Vice President
"You have a set period of time to make change happen. That's the challenge. The thrill comes when you see the results on the smiling faces of Special Olympics athletes or students attending lectures in buildings you helped bring into existence."

H. Layton "Bud" Cooper, DMin, CFRE
Executive Vice President
"Go gentle with people, make no judgments, and they respond in kind."

Robert F. Hartsook, JD, EdD
Chairman and CEO
"The big gift is available to all organizations that understand how to approach donors for their optimum commitment."

Jean Kresse
Vice President
"When you truly have a program that fits a funder's interest, the reward from a simple proposal can be hundreds of thousands of dollars."

On the Money!

MADELYN "MANDY" PONS
VICE PRESIDENT

"When you outline what makes your organization important and wonderful, how passionate you are about the work and what can be done with their support, almost everyone says, 'yes.'"

SUSAN SCHNEWEIS
SENIOR VICE PRESIDENT

"Your agency can be in business for 50 years but if the public doesn't know who you are or what you're about, it's like rowing upstream with one oar."

R. ERIC STALEY, PhD
VICE CHAIRMAN

"Money is energy that can be used for good. What I do is help bring out positive energy in support of projects that make the world a better place."

ROBERT G. SWANSON
PRESIDENT

"You can give plaques, hold dinners and send thank you cards, and you should, but in the end, communication is the essence of appreciation. People who invest in your organization simply want to hear from you."

ARLISS SWARTZENDRUBER
VICE PRESIDENT

"I enjoy encouraging people to develop skills they may not believe they have and helping them apply those skills to achieve their goals."

SUSAN DUNCAN THOMAS, CFRE
EXECUTIVE VICE PRESIDENT

"When the institution I'm representing merits support, I like asking people to support it and I like making other people feel comfortable asking for that support."

INDEX

M

N

O

P

On the Money!

About the Author

BOB HARTSOOK, JD, EdD

CHAIRMAN AND CEO

In America today, Bob Hartsook stands in the top tier among those who have influenced the scope and direction of philanthropy. His impact extends far beyond the individual organizations he has counseled and the fundraisers whose careers have been shaped by his thinking.

Bob believes that every organization deserves to have its dream tested, that people in our country really want to make a difference and that—properly prepared by organizations—they will step up to the task. Since its founding in 1987, Hartsook and Associates, now the Hartsook Companies, Inc., has conducted more than 1,200 campaigns ranging from $500,000 to more than a billion, which have raised many billions of dollars.

"The big gift is available to all organizations that understand how to approach donors for their optimum commitment," says Bob, whose Integrated Fundraising Campaign℠ National Seminar Series has introduced thousands across the country to the principles of raising capital and endowment funds while at the same time sustaining annual fund contributions so essential to an organization's long-term strength.

Bob's ability to write, teach and inspire confidence have earned a devoted audience for his seminars, books and articles. Through the years, Bob's byline has appeared in leading fundraising publications, including *The Chronicle of Philanthropy*, *The Nonprofit Times*, *Fund Raising Management* and *Planned Giving Today*. In addition, he is a regular columnist for *Philanthropy International Magazine*.

The author of more than 100 monographs published by ASR Philanthropic Publishing, Bob has also written four books. *Closing that Gift!*, now in its third printing and recommended reading by *The Chronicle of Philanthropy, CASE Currents* and other national journals, has been used widely as a training tool and required classroom text.

How to Get Million Dollar Gifts and Have Donors Thank You! has been lauded by *The Nonprofit Times* for "taking the mystery out of asking for and receiving big gifts. Think of [Bob] as Toto pulling back the curtain on the great and mighty Oz."

A best-seller at the Association of Fundraising Professionals' international conference, Bob's book, *Getting your Ducks in a Row!*, finds him collaborating with other authors to share strategies for successful campaigns.

Nobody Wants to Give Money Away! explores the nine fundraising truths essential to success through stories, humor and more than two decades of fundraising experience. The book includes illustrations by Mark Litzler, whose clever fundraising cartoons appear in *The Chronicle of Philanthropy, The Wall Street Journal*, and others.

Prior to starting the Hartsook Companies, Inc., Bob served as vice president of Colby Community College, Washburn University and Wichita State University. At Wichita State, he served as president of the board of trustees.

Bob holds a bachelor of arts in economics, a master's degree in counseling, a law degree and a doctorate in education. He has a son, Austin, who lives with him on Wrightsville Beach, North Carolina.

You may contact Dr. Hartsook at:

Dr. Robert F. Hartsook, Chairman and CEO
Hartsook Companies, Inc.
9320 E. Central, Ste. 200
Wichita, Kansas 67206
Telephone: 316.630.9992
Facsimile: 316.630.9993
email: bob@hartsookcompanies.com
Web site: www.hartsookcompanies.com

ABOUT ASR PHILANTHROPIC PUBLISHING

ASR Philanthropic Publishing serves the fundraising and philanthropic community with a variety of publications designed to inform and educate, as well as stimulate thought and discussion by professionals throughout the United States.

ASR publications include newsletters, books and monographs, as well as audio and video products. In addition, ASR's Reference Collection of monographs and books can be purchased in small or large quantities. Discounts apply to large-quantity orders. For large-quantity monograph orders, ASR can imprint your organization's logo or trademark on each copy. ASR customizes and binds collections of monographs that meet your organization's reference needs.

ASR Philanthropic Publishing has an active custom-publishing division that creates books, newsletters, brochures and other print material for use by fundraising and philanthropic organizations. The firm is available to consult on your organization's specific communication needs.

To order or receive information about any of ASR's publications or programs, please contact:

ASR Philanthropic Publishing
P.O. Box 782648
Wichita, Kansas 67278
Telephone: 316.634.2100
Facsimile: 316.630.9993
email: info@ASRpublishing.com
Web site: www.ASRpublishing.com